Exercise Book Advanced Econometrics

Peter Winker

Exercise Book Advanced Econometrics

Springer Gabler

Peter Winker
Department Business Studies and Economics
Justus Liebig University Giessen
Giessen, Germany

ISBN 978-3-662-74251-8 ISBN 978-3-662-74252-5 (eBook)
https://doi.org/10.1007/978-3-662-74252-5

This Springer Gabler imprint is published by the registered company Springer-Verlag GmbH, DE, part of Springer Nature.
The registered company address is: Heidelberger Platz 3, 14197 Berlin, Germany

Preface

Econometrics is considered to be one of the core pillars of economics teaching. While there exist many excellent text books dealing with the often formally challenging aspects of econometric theory and some of the pitfalls of applied econometrics, some students complain that there are not enough options for practicing using closed and open exercise questions.

Therefore, this exercise book addresses our students' desire to have access to such a collection of exercises, some also coming with sample solutions. The book was developed in 2025, but could harvest a large number of exercises and exam questions emerging from more than 30 years of teaching econometrics at the universities of Konstanz, Mannheim, Erfurt and Giessen. I am indebted to former teaching assistants and PhD students contributing to this pool of questions, in particular to Jenny Bethäuser, Virginie Blaess, Sebastian Bredl, Dania Eugenidis, Björn Fastrich, Henning Fischer, Iris Gönsch, Daniel Grabowski, Albina Latifi, Jochen Lüdering, Mark Meyer, Viktoriia Naboka-Krell, Jana Röder, Nicola Stork, Elena Tönjes and Dennis Türk. The author also thanks Mobina Koohi for careful proofreading and suggestions for further suggestions on solutions.

Nevertheless, the author is responsible for the collection, all errors in the questions, and possibly misleading sample solutions. Any constructive feedback on such errors and other omissions would be greatly appreciated for future improvements.

Giessen, July 2026 — Peter Winker

Instructions for Use

Dear reader,

This exercise book is aimed at students, lecturers, and other interested readers who wish to deepen their knowledge of econometrics at the master level by solving practical exercises. The numbering of sections in all Chapters 1 through 4 of the exercise book directly refers to the corresponding parts of my lecture on "Advanced Econometrics". Obviously, you find a coverage of these topics also in most intermediate to advanced level text books on econometrics. However, to the best of my knowledge, there is no single textbook covering all parts at about the same level in the same sequence as in my lecture. Thus, in order to successfully complete the individual exercises, you should have gained a solid understanding of the basic principles of econometrics and may have to collect this knowledge from reading relevant chapters in different textbooks on econometrics.

Chapter 1 contains multiple choice, true or false, and fill-in-the-blank questions. These are primarily intended to quickly test your understanding of the content of the individual chapters. However, some of these questions require more in-depth reasoning or even small calculations. Solutions to all of these questions can be found in Part II, Chapter 3.

Chapter 2 deals with exercises and exam questions for in-depth study. These include calculation and comprehension questions as well as many practical examples that require the interpretation of outputs generated using econometric software such as Eviews or R. Detailed sample solutions for some of these problems can be found in the solutions Part II, Chapter 4.

I hope that you find the questions in this book helpful for a deeper understanding of econometric analysis and that you gain substantial and useful knowledge from working on exercises for different aspects of econometrics and its applications.

Contents

Part I

Exercises

1

Single Choice Questions

This chapter provides single choice, true or false, and fill-in-the-blank questions. The single choice questions, as well as the true or false questions, have exactly one correct answer. For the fill-in-the-blank questions, you must provide the missing term(s) in the marked space.

1.0 Matrix Algebra and Principles of Inferential Statistics

Matrix Algebra

1.0.1. `Single Choice`

Consider the following matrix expressions. For which of them is the solution **not** equal to 42? Note that $\text{rk}(A)$ stands for the rank of matrix A, often also denoted as $\text{rank}(A)$.

a) $(1\ 2\ 3\ 4\ 4)(1\ 2\ 3\ 4\ 3)'$. .... ○

b) $\text{trace}\begin{pmatrix} 16 & 42 & 13 \\ 2 & 25 & 17 \\ 9 & 4 & 1 \end{pmatrix}$. .... ○

c) $\text{trace}\left((1\ 2\ 3\ 4\ 4)'(1\ 2\ 3\ 4\ 3)\right)$ .... ○

d) $\text{rk}\begin{pmatrix} 16 & 42 & 13 \\ 2 & 25 & 17 \\ 9 & 4 & 1 \end{pmatrix}$ .... ○

1.0.2. `Fill-in-the-blank`

If a matrix A satisfies the property that $AA = A$, it is called .... A matrix B with entries $b_{i,j}$ satisfying $b_{i,j} = b_{j,i}$ for all i, j is called ....

P. Winker, *Exercise Book Advanced Econometrics*,
https://doi.org/10.1007/978-3-662-74252-5_1

1.0.3. `Single Choice`

Which of the following statements is wrong?

a) $2\begin{pmatrix}5 & 7\\ 2 & 3\end{pmatrix} = \begin{pmatrix}10 & 14\\ 2 & 3\end{pmatrix}$. ○

b) $\begin{pmatrix}3 & 2 & 1\\ 1 & 2 & 3\end{pmatrix}\begin{pmatrix}5 & 8\\ 3 & 6\\ 1 & 7\end{pmatrix} = \begin{pmatrix}22 & 43\\ 14 & 41\end{pmatrix}$. ○

c) $\text{trace}\begin{pmatrix}3 & 2\\ 1 & 2\end{pmatrix} = 5$ ○

d) $\text{rk}\begin{pmatrix}5 & 8\\ 10 & 4\end{pmatrix} = 2$ ○

1.0.4. `Single Choice`

Which of the following statements is correct?

a) The addition of two matrices A and B is always defined. ○
b) The multiplication of a scalar λ with a matrix B is always defined. ○
c) The multiplication of two matrices A and B is always defined. ○
d) The inverse of a matrix A is always defined. ○

1.0.5. `True or False`

Is the following matrix idempotent?

$$A = \begin{pmatrix}2 & -2 & -4\\ -1 & 3 & 4\\ 1 & -2 & -3\end{pmatrix}$$

a) True ○
b) False ○

1.0.6. `Single Choice`

Consider the following matrices:

$$A = \begin{pmatrix}-2 & 3\\ 1 & 4\end{pmatrix}; \qquad B = \begin{pmatrix}2 & -2 & 1 & 1\\ 3 & 8 & -7 & 4\end{pmatrix}; \qquad C = \begin{pmatrix}-1 & 3\\ 8 & 2\\ 1 & -7\\ -3 & 4\end{pmatrix}$$

Which of the following statements is **not** correct?

a) AB is a 2×4 matrix. ○
b) $2AC'$ is a 2×4 matrix. ○
c) $ABB'(BB')^{-1}C'$ is a 2×4 matrix. ○
d) $AB'BC$ is a 2×4 matrix. ○

Principles of Inferential Statistics

1.0.7. `Single Choice`

Which of the following statements is correct for a given random sample of a random variable X?

a) The t-statistic for the null hypothesis $\mu = 0$, where μ stands for the expected value of X, can only be calculated if the random variable follows a normal distribution. .... ○

b) If X follows a normal distribution, the t-statistic for the null hypothesis $H_0 : \mu = 0$ calculated based on the sample mean and sample variance will follow a t-distribution with $N - 1$ degrees of freedom, where N is the number of observations in the sample. .... ○

c) For large values of N, the t-statistic is always smaller than 1.96 in absolute terms. .... ○

d) The t-statistic can only take positive values; if it is larger than 1.96, the null hypothesis must be rejected. .... ○

1.0.8. `Single Choice`

You calculated a t-statistic to test a null hypothesis about the expected value μ of a random variable $X \sim N(\mu, \sigma^2)$ based on a sample of size $N = 20$. Which of the following statements is correct?

a) The higher the absolute value of the t-statistic, the smaller the p-value. ○

b) The lower the absolute value of the t-statistic, the smaller the p-value. .... ○

c) The p-value is a linear function of the t-statistic. .... ○

d) The p-value can be obtained from the inverse of the cumulative standard normal distribution. .... ○

1.0.9. `Single Choice`

Which of the following distributions is **not** symmetric?

a) The standard normal distribution. .... ○

b) The t-distribution with 5 degrees of freedom. .... ○

c) The χ^2-distribution with 5 degrees of freedom. .... ○

d) The uniform distribution on $[-1, 1]$. .... ○

1.0.10. `Fill-in-the-blank`

The fact that a sum of identically and independently distributed random variables with finite variance converges to a normal distribution with an increasing number of summands is the content of the ....

The .... states that the empirical distribution function of draws from a random variable with finite variance converges pointwise to the theoretical distribution function of the random variable.

1.1 Aspects of (Micro)econometric Analyses

The Role of Econometrics

1.1.1. `Single Choice`

Which of the following tasks is **not** related to a central goal of econometric analysis?

a) Quantify the parameters of an economic relationship. .... ○
b) Develop a theory about the link between the income and expenditures of individuals. .... ○
c) Validate distributional assumptions. .... ○
d) Select a suitable model based on the data. .... ○

1.1.2. `Single Choice`

Which of the following ingredients is **not** always required for econometric analyzes?

a) Specific econometric software. .... ○
b) Economic theory. .... ○
c) Data. .... ○
d) Statistical/econometric methods. .... ○

1.1.3. `Single Choice`

When describing the difference between structural and reduced form models, which of the following statements is correct?

a) Reduced form models require more stringent assumptions than structural models. .... ○
b) Reduced form models cover all causal relationships explicitly. .... ○
c) It is never possible to obtain estimates of structural parameters from reduced form models. .... ○
d) Structural models are derived from theory, including strong assumptions. .... ○

1.1.4. `Single Choice`

When modeling weekly working time of employees based on a reduced form linear model including variables about education, age, and gender of the persons, which of the following potential issues should **not** affect the estimates of the impact of education?

a) Individuals with the same education, age, and sex might have different weekly working times. ○
b) Many other relevant factors, such as experience or household composition (small children), might affect weekly working time. This might result in confounding. ○
c) A linear model might not be a good approximation to the underlying structural relationships. ○
d) The data is subject to selection as unemployed or self-employed are not considered. ○

What is Special about Microeconomic Data?

1.1.5. `Single Choice`

Which of the following are **not** typical examples of microdata used for econometric analysis.?

a) Binary data on employment status (employed / unemployed) for a cross section of individuals in Germany in 2024. ○
b) Expected stock index values (6 month horizon) collected from financial market analysts in a monthly survey. ○
c) Monthly observations of the CPI for Switzerland from January 1923 to October 2025. ○
d) Top censored income data for employees from social security institutions (e.g., employment agency). ○

1.1.6. `True or False`

Consider microdata collected by phone survey. If the person on the phone answering the questions is not the person to be interviewed according to the design of the survey, this is considered as a non-sampling error.

a) True ○
b) False ○

1.1.7. `Single Choice`

Which of the following properties is **not** a typical issue which might show up in particular when dealing with microdata, e.g. stemming from a survey among individuals regarding the consumption of different goods?

a) The data do not fit well with the theoretical concepts. .... ○
b) Sampling or non-sampling errors in the data. .... ○
c) Nonlinear relationships, e.g. between income and expenditure for a specific good category. .... ○
d) The distribution of variables and error terms might not be close to normal. .... ○

1.1.8. `True or False`

Without further assumptions, the results obtained by econometric analysis provide conditional correlations that do not always imply causality.

a) True .... ○
b) False .... ○

1.1.9. `Single Choice`

Which of the following statements about the potential exogeneity of a variable is **not** correct?

a) The exogeneity of a variable is always a function of the specific analysis/model. .... ○
b) The assumption of exogeneity might be derived from economic theory. .... ○
c) The exogeneity might result from a ("natural") experiment. .... ○
d) The exogeneity can be given only for the characteristics of individuals, which cannot change over time. .... ○

1.2 Estimation

Ordinary Least Squares

1.2.1. `Single Choice`

Consider the following linear model:

$$\mathbf{Y} = \beta \mathbf{X} + \mathbf{u}\,.$$

You want to demonstrate formally that the ordinary least squares estimator $\hat{\beta}$ of β has the `BLUE` properties. Which of the following assumptions is **not** required for this proof?

a) The $\mathbf{u}$ are normally distributed. .... ○
b) $\mathbf{X}$ and $\mathbf{u}$ are not correlated. .... ○
c) The linear functional form is correct. .... ○
d) The $\mathbf{u}$ are homoskedastic. .... ○

1.2.2. `Single Choice`

Consider the following static linear model (i.e., **X** does not include lagged values of **Y**):

$$\mathbf{Y} = \beta\mathbf{X} + \mathbf{u}\,.$$

You want to demonstrate formally that the ordinary least squares estimator $\hat{\beta}$ of β has the property `U` out of the `BLUE` properties. Which of the following assumptions is required for this proof?

a) The **u** are normally distributed. ○
b) **X** and **u** are not correlated. ○
c) The **u** are uncorrelated. ○
d) The **u** are homoskedastic. ○

1.2.3. `Single Choice`

Consider the following linear model:

$$\mathbf{Y} = \beta\mathbf{X} + \mathbf{u}\,.$$

You want to demonstrate formally that the ordinary least squares estimator $\hat{\beta}$ of β has all the `BLUE` properties. Which of the following assumptions is **not** required for this proof?

a) **X** and **u** are not correlated. ○
b) The linear functional form is correct. ○
c) The **u** are homoskedastic. ○
d) The **u** are normally distributed. ○

1.2.4. `Single Choice`

Assumptions about the error terms **u** in the linear model

$$\mathbf{Y} = \beta\mathbf{X} + \mathbf{u}\,.$$

are often summarized using the notation $u \overset{iid}{\sim} N(0, \sigma_u^2)$. Which of the following assumptions is **not** covered by this notation?

a) The **u** are normally distributed. ○
b) The **u** are homoskedastic. ○
c) The **u** are efficient. ○
d) The **u** are not autocorrelated. ○

1.2.5. `Single Choice`

Consider the linear model

$$\mathbf{Y} = \beta\mathbf{X} + \mathbf{u}\,.$$

Assume that all standard assumptions for the linear regression model are satisfied (including a normal distribution of $\mathbf{u}$), but the variance-covariance matrix of the error terms $\mathbf{u}$ is known to be a diagonal matrix Ω, which has different entries on the diagonal.

Then, which of the following statements about the OLS estimator $\hat{\beta}_{OLS}$ is **not** correct?

a) $\hat{\beta}_{OLS}$ is efficient. .... ○
b) $\hat{\beta}_{OLS}$ is unbiased. .... ○
c) $\hat{\beta}_{OLS}$ is consistent. .... ○
d) $\hat{\beta}_{OLS}$ is normally distributed. .... ○

1.2.6. `Single Choice`

If the value of the coefficient of determination R^2 is less than 0.25 (25%), then ...

a) ... this indicates the presence of substantial heteroskedasticity of the error terms. .... ○
b) ... at least one additional explanatory variable must be added to the model for the OLS estimator to have the `BLUE` properties. .... ○
c) ... endogeneity of at least one regressor is likely to be present. ...... ○
d) ... None of the above statements is correct. .... ○

1.2.7. `True or False`

In a linear regression model estimated by OLS, R^2 cannot decrease when additional variables are added.

a) True .... ○
b) False .... ○

1.2.8. `Single Choice`

The value of the coefficient of determination R^2 for the linear regression model $Y_i = \beta_1 + \beta_2 X_i + u_i$ will be approximately zero if ...

a) ... the values of Y_i and X_i are small. .... ○
b) ... the value of β_1 is close to zero. .... ○
c) ... the values of u_i are small. .... ○
d) ... the variance of Y_i is similar to the variance of u_i. .... ○

1.2.9. `Single Choice`

Figure 1.1 shows four scatterplots of bivariate datasets. To each of these datasets, a linear regression model was fitted and the corresponding R^2 calculated. Which of the following orderings best corresponds to the models in terms of their R^2 values ($A > B$ means that R^2 for dataset A is greater than for dataset B).

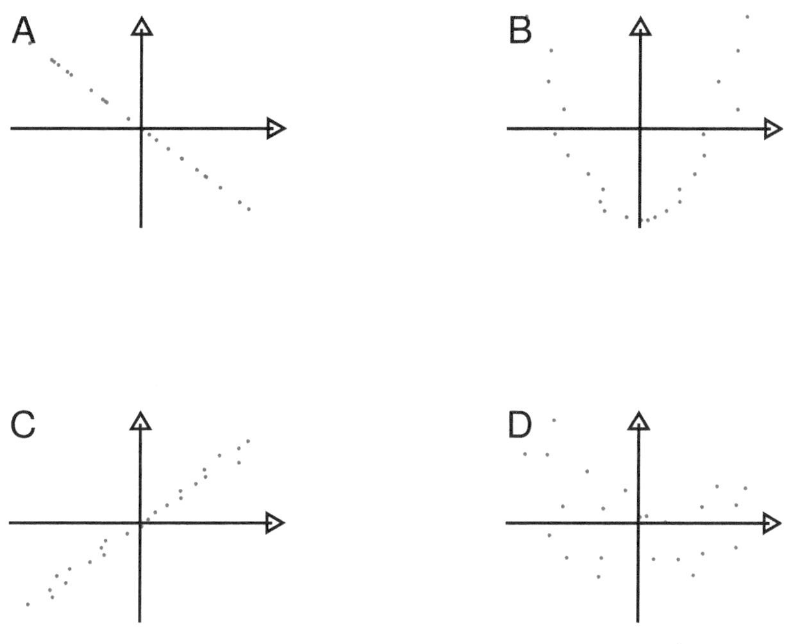

Fig. 1.1. Bivariate scatterplots.

a) $A > C > D > B$. .... ○
b) $C > A > B > D$. .... ○
c) $B > A > C > D$. .... ○
d) $C > D > B > A$. .... ○

1.2.10. `Single Choice`

Figure 1.2 shows the output of a ordinary least squares estimation for explaining the gross monthly wage `WAGE_M` of employed individuals. The only explanatory variable is age (in years) `AGE` of the person. The `C` in the column 'Variable' stands for the constant in the linear model.

```
Dependent Variable: WAGE_M          Method: Least Squares
Observations: 14837
------------------------------------------------------------
Variable   Coefficient   Std. Error   t-Statistic   Prob.
------------------------------------------------------------
C             1390.409     98.62296      14.09822   0.0000
AGE           37.96479     2.152473      17.63776   0.0000
------------------------------------------------------------
```

Fig. 1.2. Estimation output for gross monthly wages (GSOEP 2019).

Based on the results of the regression exhibited in Figure 1.2, which of the following statements is correct?

a) An increase of age by one year is associated with an increase of expected monthly gross wage of about €37.96. .... ○
b) The mean monthly gross wage of the 14 837 individuals is €1390.41. ○
c) Since age is an exogenous variable, there is no risk of confounding in this model. .... ○
d) Given the large number of observations (14 837), it can be assumed that the error terms of the linear model are normally distributed. .... ○

Nonlinear Least Squares

1.2.11. `Single Choice`

Which of the following statements about a model, which is estimated by means of nonlinear least squares (`NLS`), is **not** correct?

a) The functional relationship might be non-linear in the parameters β. . ○
b) The objective function is a non-linear function of the squared residuals. .... ○
c) Standard inference based on the t-statistic is only valid asymptotically. ○
d) The R^2 can be interpreted in a meaningful way. .... ○

1.2.12. `Single Choice`

Which of the following relationships cannot be estimated by `OLS` possibly after some transformation (such as ln or square root)?

a) $y_i = \beta_0 + \beta_1 x_i + \beta_2 x_i^3 + u_i$. .... ○
b) $y_i = \left[\beta_1 x_{1,i}^{\beta_3} + \beta_2 x_{2,i}^{\beta_3}\right]^{1/\beta_3} + u_i$. .... ○
c) $y_i = \alpha_0 x_{1,i}^{\alpha_1} x_{2,i}^{\alpha_2} u_i$. .... ○
d) $y_i^2 = \alpha_1 + 2\alpha_1\alpha_2 x_i + \alpha_2^2 x_i^2 + 2\alpha_1 u_i + 2\alpha_2 x_i u_i + u_i^2$. .... ○

1.2.13. `Single Choice`

Figure 1.3 provides the output of estimating a model that puts the two variables private consumption (`CONSUMPTION`, C_t) and disposable income (`DISP_INCOME`, Y_t^d) in relation to each other using EViews 14.

```
Dependent Variable: CONSUMPTION^2
Method: Least Squares (Gauss-Newton / Marquardt steps)
Sample: 1991Q1 2025Q2        Included observations: 138
Convergence achieved after 9 iterations
CONSUMPTION^2=  C(1)^2+2*C(1)*C(2)*DISP_INCOME
              + C(2)^2*DISP_INCOME^2
------------------------------------------------------
Variable  Coefficient  Std. Error  t-Statistic  Prob.
------------------------------------------------------
C(1)         2.190086    4.422875     0.495172   0.6213
C(2)         0.885335    0.009294     95.25702   0.0000
------------------------------------------------------
```

Fig. 1.3. Estimation output for consumption equation.

Which of the following statements regarding this estimate is **not** correct?

a) The model was estimated using non-linear least squares and employing a numerical method to solve the optimization problem. .... ○

b) The estimated model was $C_t^2 = \alpha_1 + 2\alpha_1\alpha_2 Y_i^d + \alpha_2 \left(Y_i^d\right)^2$. .... ○

c) The estimate $\hat{\alpha}_2 = 0.8853$ suggests that an increase in disposable income of € 1 is related to an increase in private consumption of €0.8853.... ○

d) The two estimates $\hat{\alpha}_1$ and $\hat{\alpha}_2$ could have been obtained more easily using `OLS`. .... ○

Generalized Least Squares

1.2.14. `Single Choice`

Consider the linear model

$$\mathbf{Y} = \beta \mathbf{X} + \mathbf{u}\,.$$

Assume that all standard assumptions for the linear regression model are satisfied, but the variance-covariance matrix of the error terms $\mathbf{u}$ is known to be a diagonal matrix Ω, which has different entries on the diagonal. Furthermore, assume that the following Cholesky-decomposition holds for the inverse of Ω:

$$\Omega^{-1} = (\Omega^{-1/2})'\Omega^{-1/2}\,.$$

Then, which of the following statements is correct?

a) The $\mathbf{u}$ are homoskedastic. ○
b) The transformed error terms $\Omega^{-1/2}\mathbf{u}$ are homoskedastic. ○
c) The transformed error terms $\Omega^{-1/2}\mathbf{u}$ are heteroskedastic. ○
d) The transformed error terms $\Omega^{-1/2}\mathbf{u}$ are not identified. ○

1.2.15. `Single Choice`

In a linear model $\mathbf{y} = \beta\mathbf{X} + \mathbf{u}$, you try to explain the monthly wage `WAGE_M` of employed people in Germany with incomes between € 1,000 and € 10,000 by the variables weekly working time in hours `WORKTIME` and `AGE` in years. The individuals included in the sample are between 20 and 65 years old.

After running the regression, you realize that the variance of the residuals increases with the age of the person. Therefore, you calculate the empirical variance of the residuals for each age 20, . . . , 65 and define an $N \times N$ diagonal matrix $\hat{\Omega}$, in which each entry $\hat{\omega}_{ii}$ corresponds to the estimated variance of residuals for the age of individual i.

Finally, you re-estimate the parameters β of the model using the formula $\hat{\beta} = \left(\mathbf{X}'\hat{\Omega}^{-1}\mathbf{X}\right)^{-1}\mathbf{X}'\hat{\Omega}^{-1}\mathbf{y}$

Which of the following statements is correct in describing your procedure?

a) There is evidence for heteroskedasticiy. Therefore, you applied a GLS estimator based on the known structure of the variance-covariance matrix $\boldsymbol{\Omega}$. ○
b) To deal with heteroskedastic errors, you use a second model for the squared residuals as a function of age and age squared to predict diagonal elements of $\boldsymbol{\Omega}$ and apply FGLS. ○
c) The estimator obtained by the described procedure will be identical to the original OLS estimator as the correct variance-covariance matrix $\hat{\boldsymbol{\Omega}}$ is used. ○
d) You obtain an empirical estimate of the variance-covariance matrix Ω exploiting the fact that for each age you have several observations allowing for the calculation of an age specific variance of residuals, which is used in the final FGLS estimator. ○

1.2.16. `Single Choice`

Consider the linear model

$$\mathbf{Y} = \beta\mathbf{X} + \mathbf{u}\,.$$

Assume that all standard assumptions for the linear regression model are satisfied, but $E(\mathbf{X}'\mathbf{u}) \neq \mathbf{0}$. In this situation, instrumental variables ("instruments") might be used to avoid biased estimates. Which of the following statements about good instruments $\mathbf{Z}$ is **not** correct?

a) The number of instruments has to be at least as large as the number of variables in $\mathbf{X}$. .... ○
b) The instruments should be correlated with the variables in $\mathbf{X}$. .... ○
c) The instruments should not be correlated with $\mathbf{u}$. .... ○
d) The instruments should not contain variables from $\mathbf{X}$. .... ○

1.2.17. `Single Choice`

Consider the linear model

$$\mathbf{Y} = \beta \mathbf{X} + \mathbf{u}\,.$$

Assume that all standard assumptions for the linear regression model are satisfied, but $E(\mathbf{X}'\mathbf{u}) \neq \mathbf{0}$. Assume you have good instruments $\mathbf{Z}$ for $\mathbf{X}$. Which of the following statements about possible estimation procedures is correct?

a) You can obtain unbiased estimates of β by adding $\mathbf{Z}$ to the equation above and applying OLS. .... ○
b) You can obtain unbiased estimates of β using a two-stage estimator by first regressing $\mathbf{X}$ on $\mathbf{Z}$ and replacing $\mathbf{X}$ by the forecasts from this model ($\hat{\mathbf{X}}$) in the above equation before applying OLS. .... ○
c) You can obtain unbiased estimates of β using an FGLS estimator using the estimated variance-covariance matrix $\hat{\Omega} = \mathbf{Z}\mathbf{Z}'$ of $\mathbf{u}$. .... ○
d) You cannot obtain unbiased estimates of β by any of the methods a) - c). .... ○

1.2.18. `Single Choice`

You estimate a model to explain the monthly wages of individuals. One of the explanatory variables is education measured by years of schooling (`SCHOOL_T`). You are concerned that this variable might be endogenous with regard to income, as schooling decisions might be affected by expected future wages as well as by unobserved factors like motivation. Therefore, you apply an instrumental variable approach using the highest level of schooling attained by the parents as instruments. Figure 1.4 shows the output of the first stage, i.e. when regressing `SCHOOL_T` on dummy variables for parents education.

```
Dependent Variable: SCHOOL_T
Method: Least Squares          Included observations: 1546
-------------------------------------------------------------
Variable      Coefficient   Std. Error   t-Statistic   Prob.
-------------------------------------------------------------
C                10.53088    0.045309      232.4247   0.0000
EDU_FATHER=2     0.150457    0.113383      1.326975   0.1847
EDU_FATHER=3     1.039039    0.470478      2.208474   0.0274
EDU_MOTHER=2     0.791742    0.105956      7.472373   0.0000
EDU_MOTHER=3    -0.404755    0.614705     -0.658454   0.5103
-------------------------------------------------------------
R-squared               0.0525   Mean depend. var     10.7277
Adjusted R-squared 0.0500   S.D. depend. var      1.57414
F-statistic             21.333   Prob(F-statistic)    0.00000
-------------------------------------------------------------
```

Fig. 1.4. Estimation output of first stage of IV estimator.

Which of the following statements about the first stage regression is **not** correct?

a) The positive value of the coefficient of the dummy variable that the mother has attained the second (of three levels) of education together with the corresponding t-statistic of 7.4723 indicates a positive impact of these level of education on the years of schooling of children compared to the lowest level. This effect is significantly different from 0 at the 5% level. ○

b) The low level of the adjusted R^2 of 0.0500 indicates that it is not possible to calculate the second stage of the two-stage IV estimator. .... ○

c) The value of 10.7277 is equivalent to the mean of the number of years spent in school of the individuals included in the sample. .... ○

d) The F-statistic of 21.333 corresponds to the Crack-Donald statistic for testing for weak instruments (using the critical values provided by Stock and Yugo). .... ○

Maximum Likelihood

1.2.19. `True or False`

If the dependent variable of a model can only take on discrete values (e.g. 0 and 1), the Likelihood of the model can be interpreted as probability of observing what is actually observed.

a) True .... ○

b) False .... ○

1.2.20. `Single Choice`

When comparing estimation by Ordinary Least Squares (`OLS`) and Maximum Likelihood (`ML`) with regard to the objective function, which of the following statements is **not** correct?

a) In both cases, an objective function must be maximized or minimized. .... ○
b) The objective function for `OLS` is based on observed values of the dependent variable and forecasts of the model. .... ○
c) In `ML` the objective function reflects the likelihood to observe what we observe. .... ○
d) Both estimators can be obtained by solving a system of linear equations. .... ○

1.2.21. `Single Choice`

Consider the linear model $\mathbf{y} = \mathbf{X}\beta + \mathbf{u}$ with error terms $\mathbf{u}$, which are independently identically normally distributed and not correlated with $\mathbf{X}$. The matrix $\mathbf{X}$ is assumed to include a column with ones (i.e. the model includes a constant). Thus, $u_i \overset{iid}{\sim} \mathcal{N}(0, \sigma^2)$.

Which of the following statements about the OLS estimators $(\hat{\beta}_{OLS}, \hat{\sigma^2}_{OLS})$ and maximum likelihood (ML) estimators $(\hat{\beta}_{ML}, \hat{\sigma^2}_{ML})$ of this model is correct?

a) The OLS estimators can be obtained from closed form expressions (analytically), while the calculation of the ML estimators requires numerical optimization methods. .... ○
b) Both estimators are identical. .... ○
c) Both estimators are consistent estimators of β and σ^2. .... ○
d) The ML estimator of β is more efficient than the OLS estimator. ..... ○

1.2.22. `Single Choice`

Consider the linear model $\mathbf{y} = \mathbf{X}\beta + \mathbf{u}$ with error terms $\mathbf{u}$, which are independently normally distributed and not correlated with $\mathbf{X}$. The matrix $\mathbf{X}$ is assumed to include a column with ones (i.e. the model includes a constant). Thus, $u_i \sim \mathcal{N}(0, \sigma_i^2)$, where σ_i^2 denotes the variance of the error terms for observation i. Furthermore, it is assumed that σ_i^2 is a quadratic function of an explanatory variable in $\mathbf{X}$. Let us denote this variable by z. Thus, it is assumed that $\sigma_i^2 = \alpha_0 + \alpha_1 z_i + \alpha_2 z_i^2$.

Which of the following statements is **not** correct?

a) In general, estimation by FGLS is not feasible due to the non-linear relationship between z_i and σ_i^2. .... ○
b) If the function of z_i for σ_i^2 is just a constant, i.e., $\alpha_1 = 0$ and $\alpha_2 = 0$, the model can be efficiently estimated by OLS. .... ○
c) Parameters β can be consistently estimated both by FGLS and by ML. ○
d) ML allows to estimate β and parameters of the quadratic function linking z_i and σ_i^2 in one step. .... ○

1.2.23. `Single Choice`

Consider a linear model of expenditures for renting an apartment, depending – among other factors – on monthly wage income. It is assumed that the error terms u_i are heteroskedastic, and that the variance σ_i^2 of u_i depends on the wage income w_i: $\sigma_i^2 = \alpha_1 + \alpha_2 w_i^{\gamma}$. All parameters of the model except γ are estimated using a maximum likelihood estimator. Figure 1.5 shows the plot of the resulting log-Likelihood values (y-axis) for different preset values of γ (x-axis).

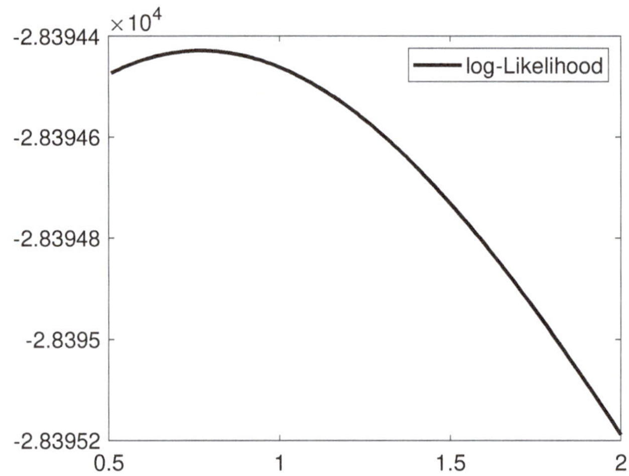

Fig. 1.5. Log-likelihood function.

Based on this information, which of the following statements is correct?

a) When including γ in the maximum likelihood estimation as a parameter, the estimated value should be between 0.5 and 1. .... ○
b) The figure is flawed because negative values are not possible for the log-likelihood function. .... ○
c) The figure indicates that the optimal value of the exponent γ is close to 2. .... ○
d) The shape of the curve resembles that of a normal density function close to its maximum. Therefore, the assumption of a normal distribution of the error terms u_i can be confirmed. .... ○

Generalized Method of Moments

1.2.24. Single Choice

When comparing estimation by General Method of Moments (GMM) and Maximum Likelihood(ML) with regard to the objective function, which of the following statements is correct?

a) In both cases, an objective function must be maximized. .... ○
b) In ML the objective function reflects the likelihood to observe what we observe. .... ○
c) In GMM the objective function does not depend on the explanatory variables **X**. .... ○
d) While the objective function for ML, in general, is non-linear, the objective function for GMM is linear. .... ○

1.2.25. Single Choice

Consider the linear model

$$\mathbf{Y} = \beta\mathbf{X} + \mathbf{u}\,.$$

Assume that all standard assumptions for the linear regression model are satisfied, but the variance-covariance matrix of the error terms $\mathbf{u}$ is known to be a diagonal matrix Ω, which has different entries on the diagonal. Furthermore, assume that the following Cholesky-decomposition holds for the inverse of Ω:

$$\Omega^{-1} = (\Omega^{-1/2})'\Omega^{-1/2}\,.$$

Let $\hat{\beta}_{\mathbf{OLS}}$ denote the OLS estimator of the model above and $\hat{\beta}_{\mathbf{GMM}}$ the GMM estimator based on the moment conditions $E(\mathbf{X}'\mathbf{u}) = \mathbf{0}$. When applying the OLS estimator on the transformed model

$$\Omega^{-1/2}Y = \Omega^{-1/2}X + \Omega^{-1/2}u\,,$$

one obtains an estimator $\hat{\beta}_?$. Which of the following statements is correct for this estimator?

a) $\hat{\beta}_? = \hat{\beta}_{\mathbf{OLS}}$. .... ○
b) $\hat{\beta}_? = \hat{\beta}_{\mathbf{GMM}}$. .... ○
c) $\hat{\beta}_? = \mathbf{1} - \hat{\beta}_{\mathbf{OLS}}$. .... ○
d) $\hat{\beta}_? = \hat{\beta}_{\mathbf{GLS}}$. .... ○

1.2.26. Single Choice

Figure 1.6 shows the output of a GMM estimation. The variables WAGE_H and EDUCATION stand for hourly wages and years spent in education, respectively. The variables EDUC_FATHER and EDUC_MOTHER indicate the levels of higher education of the parents.

```
Dependent Variable: WAGE_H
Method: Generalized Method of Moments
Included observations: 601
Instrument specification: C EDUC_FATHER EDUC_MOTHER
-------------------------------------------------------
Variable     Coefficient   Std. Error  t-Statistic  Prob.
-------------------------------------------------------
C              -15.61623    6.869137    -2.273390  0.0234
EDUCATION       3.218576    0.675422     4.765281  0.0000
-------------------------------------------------------
```

Fig. 1.6. Generalized Method of Moments estimation output.

Based on the estimation output, which of the following statements is correct?

a) Based on this estimation approach, it is not possible to test for over-identifying restrictions. ○
b) The number of instruments used was smaller than the number of variables in the model. ○
c) Estimation of the model by means of two stage least squares (`TSLS`) would result in different estimates of the influence of `EDUCATION` on hourly wages. ○
d) The model takes into account the potential endogeneity of the time spent in education by using an instrumental variable approach. ○

1.3 Hypothesis Testing and Model Selection

Linear Hypothesis

1.3.1. `Single Choice`

Consider the following linear model and assume that all relevant assumptions about the model are satisfied.

$$Y_t = \beta_0 + \beta_1 X_{1,t} + \beta_2 X_{2,t} + \ldots + \beta_k X_{k,t} + u_t \, , t = 1, \ldots, 21$$

Which of the following hypotheses **cannot** be analyzed using standard t- or F-tests?

a) H_0^1: $\beta_2 = 1$ ○
b) H_0^2: $\beta_1/\beta_2 = 3$ ○
c) H_0^3: $\beta_1\beta_2 = 0.4$ ○
d) H_0^4: $\beta_1 = \beta_2 = \ldots = \beta_k = 0$ ○

1.3.2. `Single Choice`

Consider the following linear model and assume that all relevant assumptions about the model are satisfied.

$$Y_t = \beta_0 + \beta_1 X_{1,t} + \beta_2 X_{2,t} + \beta_3 X_{3,t} + \beta_4 X_{4,t} + u_t \,, t = 1, \ldots, 25$$

You are interested in testing the hypothesis H_0: $\beta_2 = 0$ and $\beta_3 = 0$, and want to write the null hypothesis in the form $R\beta - r = 0$. Which of the following statements regarding R and r is correct?

a) The dimension of R is 1×5 and r is a scalar 0. .... ○

b) $R = \begin{bmatrix} 0\,0\,1\,0\,0 \\ 0\,0\,0\,1\,0 \end{bmatrix}$ and r is a scalar 0. .... ○

c) $R = \begin{bmatrix} 0\;0\;1\;-1\;0 \end{bmatrix}$ and r is a scalar 0. .... ○

d) The dimension of R is 2×5. .... ○

1.3.3. Assume all model assumptions are satisfied both for the Ordinary Least Squares (`OLS`) and the Maximum Likelihood (`ML`) estimator. The sample size is N and the number of estimated coefficients is K. Which of the following statements is correct with regard to the interpretation of the t-statistic calculated for the null hypothesis $\beta_1 = 0$ based on the estimators?

a) If $N - K > 5$ and the t-statistic is greater than 2.6, the null hypothesis can be rejected at the 5% level for the `OLS` estimator. .... ○

b) The t-statistic follows a t-distribution with $N - K$ degrees of freedom for the `ML` estimator. .... ○

c) The t-statistic follows a t-distribution with N degrees of freedom for the `OLS` estimator. .... ○

d) For both estimators, the distribution of the t-statistic is known only asymptotically. .... ○

1.3.4. Figure 1.7 shows the output of an OLS estimation. The variables `WAGE_M` and `WORKTIME` stand for monthly gross wages and weekly working hours, respectively.

```
Dependent Variable: WAGE_M          Method: Least Squares
Included observations: 8466
------------------------------------------------------------
Variable     Coefficient   Std. Error t-Statistic   Prob.
------------------------------------------------------------
C               446.7304     67.52848     6.615437   0.0000
WORKTIME        79.92337     1.709403     46.75513   0.0000
------------------------------------------------------------
R-squared       0.205261    Mean dependent var    3486.320
F-statistic     2186.043    Prob(F-statistic)     0.000000
------------------------------------------------------------
```

Fig. 1.7. Ordinary Least Squares estimation output.

Based on the estimation output, which of the following statements is **not** correct?

a) It is a random result that the t-statistic for the null hypothesis that the coefficient for `WORKTIME` is zero is equal to the square root of the F-statistic. ○

b) The t-statistic for the variable `WORKTIME` allows to reject the null hypothesis that the effect of `WORKTIME` on monthly wages is zero at the 5% level. ○

c) The R^2 indicates that a bit more than 20% of the variation in monthly wages can be described based on the variation in weekly working time. ○

d) Increasing weekly working time by one more hour will ceteris paribus be linked with an increase of expected monthly wages of about € 79.92. ○

1.3.5. Figure 1.8 shows the output of an OLS estimate. The variables `CONSUMPTION` and `DISP_INCOME` stand for quarterly private consumption and disposable income, respectively. `@SEAS(1)`, `@SEAS(2)`, and `@SEAS(3)` are seasonal dummies for the first to third quarter. Finally, `R3M` is the three month money market rate, i.e. a short term interest rate, while `R9Y` is an interest rate for long-term (9 years) bonds.

Assume that all assumptions for the ordinary linear regression model are satisfied and that the level of statistical significance is set at 5%. Based on the estimation output, which of the following statements is **not** correct?

a) Consumption in the first quarter is – ceteris paribus – statistically significantly lower than in the reference quarter four. ○

b) The marginal effect of income on consumption is – ceteris paribus – statistically significantly different from 1. ○

c) The marginal effect of the short term interest rate `R3M` is – ceteris paribus – not statistically significantly different from zero. ○

d) The effect of interest rates is – ceteris paribus – not statistically significant (different from zero). ○

```
Dependent Variable: CONSUMPTION  Method: Least Squares
Sample: 1993Q1 2007Q4      Included observations: 60
-----------------------------------------------------
Variable    Coefficient  Std. Error t-Statistic  Prob.
-----------------------------------------------------
C               7.580042    7.388566    1.025915  0.3096
@SEAS(1)       -16.21932    0.768333   -21.10975  0.0000
@SEAS(2)       -2.493588    0.788335   -3.163107  0.0026
@SEAS(3)        0.811112    0.779963    1.039937  0.3031
DISP_INCOME     0.901954    0.015574    57.91288  0.0000
R3M            -0.396614    0.273295   -1.451228  0.1526
R9Y            -0.985714    0.506554   -1.945922  0.0570
-----------------------------------------------------
F-statistic   2475.0634      Prob(F-statistic)  0.0000
-----------------------------------------------------
```

Fig. 1.8. Ordinary Least Squares estimation output.

1.3.6. Figure 1.8 shows the output of an OLS estimate. The variables `CONSUMPTION` and `DISP_INCOME` stand for quarterly private consumption and disposable income, respectively. `@SEAS(1)`, `@SEAS(2)`, and `@SEAS(3)` are seasonal dummies for the first to third quarter. Finally, `R3M` is the three month money market rate, i.e. a short term interest rate, while `R9Y` is an interest rate for long-term (9 years) bonds.

Assume that all assumptions for the ordinary linear regression model are satisfied and that the level of statistical significance is set at 5%.. Based on the estimation output, which of the following statements is correct?

a) The null hypothesis that there are no seasonal effects can be rejected based on the large F-statistics. . . . . ○

b) The large F-statistics indicates that the null hypothesis "all explanatory variables together have no explanatory power" has to be rejected. . . . . ○

c) The null hypothesis that the marginal effect of disposable income is statistically significantly different from zero cannot be rejected. . . . . ○

d) The null hypothesis that the marginal effect of `R3M` is statistically significantly different from zero has to be rejected. . . . . ○

1.3.7. Based on the estimates shown in Figure 1.8, an F-Test on the coefficients corresponding to the seasonal dummies `@SEAS(1)`, `@SEAS(2)`, and `@SEAS(3)` was conducted. The null hypothesis was that all three coefficients are equal to zero. The results are shown in Figure 1.9.

Test Statistic	Value	df	Probability
F-statistic	221.1538	(3,53)	0.0000

Fig. 1.9. Results of F-test for linear regression model.

Assume that all assumptions for the ordinary linear regression model are satisfied and that the level of statistical significance is set at 5%. Which of the following statements regarding these results is **not** correct?

a) The 3 in $(3, 53)$ reflects that an assumption about three coefficients is tested. ○
b) The small probability value (< 0.0001) indicates that the null hypothesis has to be rejected. ○
c) The F-statistic is much smaller than the one shown in Figure 1.8. Thus, the null hypothesis cannot be rejected. ○
d) The null hypothesis corresponds to a situation where there are – ceteris paribus – no seasonal patterns in consumption. ○

General Hypothesis

1.3.8. Single Choice

When conducting tests of general hypotheses $c(\theta) = \mathbf{0}$ in a Maximum Likelihood setting, there are three different procedures available. Which of the following tests does **not** belong to these procedures?

a) Wald-test. ○
b) Forest-test. ○
c) Likelihood-ratio test. ○
d) Lagrange-multiplier-test. ○

1.3.9. Single Choice

When conducting tests of general hypotheses $c(\theta) = \mathbf{0}$ in a Maximum Likelihood setting, different procedures are available. What is the main drawback of the Likelihood-ratio test compared to alternative approaches such as Wald-test or Lagrange-multiplier test, when $c(\theta)$ is a non-linear function?

a) For the likelihood-ratio test, both estimates of the unrestricted and restricted models are required. ○
b) For the likelihood-ratio test, $c(\theta)$ has to be a polynomial function. ○
c) The distribution of the likelihood-ratio test statistic under the null hypothesis is known only asymptotically. ○
d) The likelihood-ratio test statistic can only be calculated if $c(\hat{\theta}) \neq \mathbf{0}$. ○

1.3.10. Single Choice

When all assumptions including normality of the error terms are satisfied for a linear model, the estimates of the parameters β by OLS and ML are identical. Assume a sample size of $N = 50$. Which of the following statements is correct in such a setting?

a) Calculating t-statistics for individual coefficients β_k based on the OLS and ML estimators provides numerically identical values. .... ○

b) The distribution of the F-statistic for testing a linear hypothesis on β is only known asymptotically. .... ○

c) It is possible to test non-linear restrictions on the parameter vector β by means of the Wald-test with an asymptotically chi^2-distributed test statistic. .... ○

d) The distribution of test statistics for non-linear restrictions is known to be the F-statistic with k and $N - K$ degrees of freedom, where k denotes the number of restrictions and K the number of estimated parameters. ... ○

1.3.11. Single Choice

Figure 1.10 provides a schematic presentation of testing general hypotheses in a maximum likelihood estimation problem. The left axis shows values of the log-likelihood function $lnL(\theta)$ exhibited as the black line, while the right axis shows values of a non-linear constraint function $c(\theta)$ presented by the dashed blue line. The ML estimator is $\hat{\theta}_M L$, which is also labeled as an unconstrained estimator $\hat{\theta}_U$, while the parameter value satisfying the constraint $c(\theta) = 0$ is labeled $\hat{\theta}_R$.

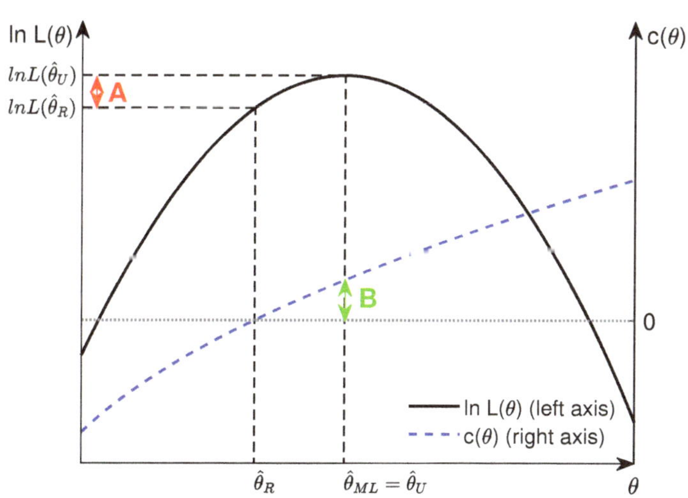

Fig. 1.10. Schematic outline of general hypothesis testing in ML.

The figure also exhibits two distances marked by double arrows and labeled **A** and **B**, respectively. Which of the following statements is correct with respect to this figure?

a) The difference between the distances marked **A** and **B** corresponds to the Lagrange multiplier (LM) statistic for the null hypothesis $H_0 : c(\theta) = 0$. .... ○

b) The distance marked **A** is proportional to the value of the likelihood ratio (LR) statistic for the null hypothesis $H_0 : c(\theta) = 0$. .... ○

c) The distance marked **B** is proportional to the value of the Wald statistic for the null hypothesis $H_0 : c(\theta) = 0$. .... ○

d) None of the statements a) – c) is correct. .... ○

1.3.12. Single Choice

Figure 1.11 shows the results of running a Wald test on the null hypothesis that two coefficients in a linear regression model with seven parameters are simultaneously zero, i.e., $H_0 : \beta_6 = 0$ and $\beta_7 = 0$.

Wald Test

Test Statistic	Value	df	Probability
F-statistic	5.359368	(2, 53)	0.0076
Chi-square	10.71874	2	0.0047

Fig. 1.11. Results of Wald test for linear regression model.

Which of the following statements on this output is **not** correct?

a) The F-statistic provides exact inference if all assumptions (including normal distribution of the error terms) for OLS are satisfied. .... ○

b) If all assumptions for ML estimation (including the correct, but not necessarily normal distributional assumption about the error terms) are satisfied, the `Chi-square` (χ^2) statistic can be interpreted asymptotically. .... ○

c) If one of the assumptions described in a) and b) holds and one assumes that the sample size of $N = 60$ is rather large, one would reject the null hypothesis at the level of 5%. .... ○

d) Since the null hypothesis is linear, the `Chi-square` (χ^2) statistic cannot be used. .... ○

Hypothesis about Model Assumptions

1.3.13. `Single Choice`

For the relationship between a dependent variable **Y** and explanatory variables **X**, a linear model

$$\mathbf{Y} = \beta\mathbf{X} + \mathbf{u}$$

is assumed. The observations in the sample are ordered by time. You are concerned that the linear model might not be appropriate for this specific application. Which of the following approaches is **not** helpful to inform you about this risk?

a) The Jarque-Bera statistic calculated based on the residuals of the estimated model. .... ○
b) The Ramsey reset test. .... ○
c) Splitting the sample in two halves and comparing estimates for the two sub-samples. .... ○
d) Analyzing a plot of the estimated residuals over time. .... ○

1.3.14. `Single Choice`

Based on quarterly data for Germany from 1960.1 to 2024.4 (for West Germany until 1990.4 and unified Germany from 1991.1 onward), a consumption function was estimated. The dependent variable private consumption was modeled as a linear function of a constant, disposable income, and three seasonal dummies. As part of testing the assumptions of the linear model, a Chow breakpoint test was conducted with EViews. The test results are shown in Figure 1.12.

```
Chow Breakpoint Test: 1991Q1
Null Hypothesis: No breaks at specified breakpoints
Equation Sample: 1960Q1 2024Q4
------------------------------------------------------
F-statistic            21.7520  Prob. F(5,250)        0.0000
Log likel. ratio       93.9101  Prob. Chi-Square(5)   0.0000
Wald Statistic        108.7600  Prob. Chi-Square(5)   0.0000
------------------------------------------------------
```

Fig. 1.12. Results of Chow breakpoint test for linear regression model.

Which of the following statements regarding the test results is **not** correct?

a) The null hypothesis of the test is no structural break in 1991.1. ...... ○
b) The F-statistic should be used if the error terms are normally distributed. .... ○
c) LR test (based on Log likel. ratio) and Wald test (based on Wald statistic) suggest that there is no structural break. .... ○
d) For large sample sizes (asymptotically), LR test and Wald test will provide the same conclusion. .... ○

1.3.15. `Single Choice`

Assume that you consider the linear model

$$\mathbf{Y} = \beta\mathbf{X} + \mathbf{u}$$

and want to test the assumption that the error terms **u** are independently distributed, i.e., do not exhibit autocorrelation. Which of the following statements regarding such a test is correct?

a) The Jarque-Bera test based on the residuals of the estimated model can be used for this purpose. .... ○

b) The test can be based on the Durbin-Watson statistic calculated for the estimated residuals of the model. If the test statistic is larger than 2, the null hypothesis of no autocorrelation has to be rejected. .... ○

c) The test can be based on the Box-Pierce Q-statistic for autocorrelation up to order $p \geq 1$. If the test statistic is larger than the 95% quantile of the χ^2-distribution with p degrees of freedom, the null hypothesis of no autocorrelation has to be rejected at the level 5%. .... ○

d) None of the statements a) - c) is correct. .... ○

1.3.16. `Single Choice`

Which of the following suggestions is **not** a typical source of autocorrelation in a linear regression model with time series data?

a) Missing relevant variables. .... ○

b) Superfluous variables. .... ○

c) Wrong functional form. .... ○

d) Structural breaks. .... ○

1.3.17. `Single Choice`

Assume that you consider the linear model

$$\mathbf{Y} = \beta\mathbf{X} + \mathbf{u}$$

and want to test the assumption that the error terms **u** are normally distributed. Which of the following statements regarding such a test is correct?

a) The Jarque-Bera test based on the residuals of the estimated model can be used for this purpose. .... ○

b) The test can be based on the Durbin-Watson statistic calculated for the estimated residuals of the model. .... ○

c) The cumulative distribution function of u can be compared with the cumulative standard normal distribution using the Lilliefors' test. .... ○

d) None of the statements a) - c) is correct. .... ○

1.3.18. `Single Choice`

Assume that you consider the linear model

$$\mathbf{Y} = \beta \mathbf{X} + \mathbf{u}$$

and want to test the assumption that the error terms $\mathbf{u}$ are homoskedastic. Which of the following statements regarding such a test is correct?

a) The Jarque-Bera test based on the residuals of the estimated model can be used for this purpose. .... ○
b) The White-test with cross terms can be used for this purpose. .... ○
c) The cumulative distribution function of u can be compared with the cumulative standard normal distribution using the Lilliefors' test. ...... ○
d) The Breusch-Godfrey test can be used. .... ○

1.3.19. `Fill-in-the-blank`

Based on the German Socio-Economic Panel (2021), you estimated a linear regression model for rent payments as a function of monthly wages, number of children in the household, region (East/West Germany), and a dummy for smokers. You are concerned that the functional form chosen (linear) is not correct. Therefore, you want to run a test of this assumption.

A test for the null hypothesis H_0: the functional form is correct is the ....–test. Its general idea consists of adding .... of $\hat{\mathbf{Y}}_t$ to a test equation, which should not have a significant impact if H_0 is correct.

1.3.20. `Single Choice`

Figure 1.13 shows parts of the results of running a test for a linear regression model for rent payments as a function of monthly wages, the number of children in the household, the region (East/West Germany) and a dummy for smokers.

```
XXXXXX YYYYYY Test
Omitted Variables: Squares of fitted values
Specific.: RENT C WAGE_M NR_CHILD DEAST DSMOKER
------------------------------------------------
                 Value        df        Probability
F-statistic     2.5553     (1, 3054)       0.1100
------------------------------------------------
```

Fig. 1.13. Results of unlabeled test for linear regression model.

Which of the following statements on this result is **not** correct?

a) A Ramsey RESET test for the correct functional form was conducted adding squares of fitted values to the original model. ○

b) The null hypothesis that the functional form is correct has to be rejected at the 5% level. ○

c) The sample contains 3 059 observations. ○

d) The result of the test does not suggest that the model has to be modified. ○

1.3.21. Single Choice

Assume that a colleague of yours would like to estimate a wage regression with observations (individuals) taken from the German Socioeconomic Panel (GSOEP) 2021. She specifies the following linear model

$$\text{WAGE\_M}_i = \beta_0 + \beta_1\ \text{SCHOOL\_T}_i + \beta_2\ \text{AGE}_i + \beta_3\ \text{SEX}_i + \beta_4\ \text{DEAST}_i + u_i\ ,$$

where the variables are given by

WAGE_M:	monthly gross wages
SCHOOL_T:	years of schooling
AGE:	age in years
SEX:	dummy (1 = woman)
DEAST:	dummy (1 = living in East Germany)

After estimation, she runs a test on the residuals $\hat{u}_i$ of the model resulting in the following output:

```
Heteroskedasticity Test: White
----------------------------------------------------
F-statistic    100.55   Prob. F(4,6530)      0.0000
Obs*R-squared  379.14   Prob. Chi-Square(4)  0.0000
----------------------------------------------------
```

Which of the following statements on this result is **not** correct?

a) The null hypothesis of the test is that the error terms are homoskedastic. ○

b) The White-test for heteroskedasticity was run with cross terms. ○

c) The null hypothesis of the test must be rejected at the 5% level. ○

d) The sample comprises more than 6 000 observations. ○

1.3.22. Fill-in-the-blank

For a linear regression model to explain expenditures on housing RENT, an assumption was tested with respect to the error terms, resulting in the output (with some missing information highlighted by ...) in Figure 1.14.

```
------------------------------------------------------
Test: ....................
Null hypothesis: ................
------------------------------------------------------
F-statistic      3.9488    Prob. F(8,3051)       0.0001
Obs*R squared   31.3586    Prob. Chi-Square(8)   0.0001
------------------------------------------------------


------------------------------------------------------
Test Equation:               Dependent Variable: RESID^2
Method: Least Squares        Included observations: 3060
Collinear test regressors dropped from specification
------------------------------------------------------
Variable          Coefficient Std. Err. t-Stat.   Prob.
------------------------------------------------------
C                   5240290    614528   8.5273   0.0000
WAGE_M^2           -0.03554    0.0293  -1.2122   0.2255
WAGE_M*NR_CHILD     91.2935    64.348   1.4188   0.1561
WAGE_M*DSMOKER      110.868    195.25   0.5678   0.5702
WAGE_M              501.341    279.32   1.7948   0.0728
NR_CHILD^2          79254.5    114832   0.6902   0.4901
NR_CHILD*DSMOKER    -123197    334739  -0.3680   0.7129
NR_CHILD            -119653    414552  -0.2886   0.7729
DSMOKER^2           -330135    764454  -0.4319   0.6659
------------------------------------------------------
R-squared   0.010248     Mean dependent var  6760998.3
------------------------------------------------------
```

Fig. 1.14. Results of unlabeled test.

Please complete the following statement:

The output is the result of a ································–test. Thereby, the null-hypothesis is that the error terms of the model are ································. Based on the output, this null-hypothesis ······························ rejected.

1.3.23. Single Choice

After running a regression of private consumption on disposable income and three seasonal dummies for quarterly German data from 1991.1 to 2025.3, you have a look at the residuals of the regression based on the output of EViews 14 shown in Figure 1.15.

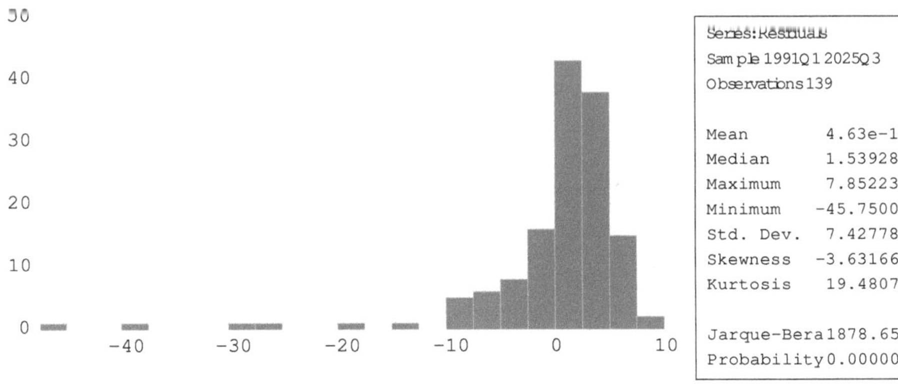

Fig. 1.15. EViews 14 output for consumption equation.

Which of the following statements can be supported by the output shown in Figure 1.15?

a) The null hypothesis of a normal distribution of the error terms has to be rejected at the 5%-level. .... ○
b) There is no indication of autocorrelation of error terms. .... ○
c) The mean of the residuals is different from zero. .... ○
d) The seasonal dummies in the model are superfluous. .... ○

1.3.24. `Single Choice`

After running a regression of private consumption on disposable income and three seasonal dummies for quarterly German data from 1991.1 to 2025.3, you produce a plot presented in Figure 1.16. The figure shows the cumulative empirical distribution of the residuals (red line) and the cumulative theoretical normal distribution with the same variance (blue line). The dashed green line indicates the values on the x-axis for which the difference between both distribution functions is maximum.

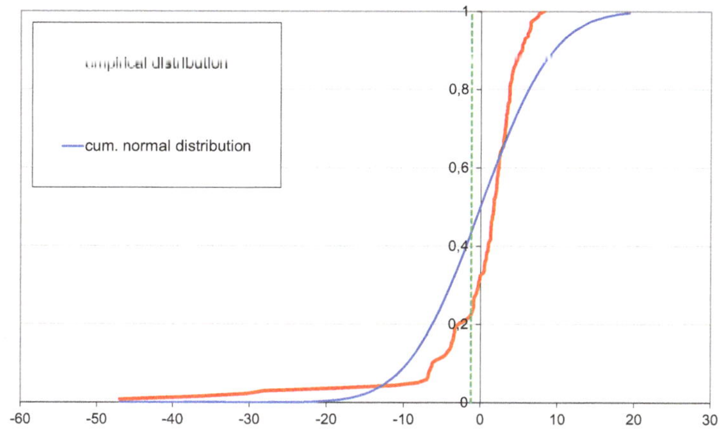

Fig. 1.16. Plots of cumulative empirical and normal distribution functions.

Which of the following statements can be supported by the output shown in Figure 1.16?

a) More than 50% of all residuals are negative. . . . . ○

b) The maximum distance between both lines corresponds to the Lilliefors statistics. . . . . ○

c) The maximum distance between both lines multiplied with the number of observations corresponds to the Jarque-Bera statistic. . . . . ○

d) If the error terms were normally distributed with the assumed variance, residual values smaller than -20 are impossible. ○

1.3.25. `Single Choice`

You estimate a linear regression model and perform a few specification tests at the 5% level, e.g., regarding correct functional form as well as homoscedasticity, no autocorrelation, and normal distribution of error terms. We assume that the model satisfies all these requirements. When you repeat the analysis for many independent samples from the model, which of the following statements is correct?

a) You will reject at least one of the null hypotheses in at least 20% of the repetitions. . . . . ○

b) You will reject at least one of the null hypotheses in not more than 20% of the repetitions. . . . . ○

c) You will reject all hypotheses in less than 0,000625% of the repetitions. . . . . ○

d) You will reject all hypotheses in more than 5% of the repetitions. . . . . ○

Model Selection

1.3.26. `Single Choice`

You are interested in a linear model that explains monthly wages as the dependent variable y. Based on an extensive review of the literature, you obtained a long list of potential influential factors x_k. Your data set comprises $N = 65$ observations for y and all x_k, $k = 1, \ldots 78$.

In a first attempt to find a good model, you compare 7 models comprising between 2 and 16 different explanatory variables. One of your colleagues suggested using the R^2 of the models considered for this purpose.

Which of the following statements is **not** correct in this setting?

a) The R^2 for a model provides the share of variation in y, which can be explained by the variation of the x variables included in the model. .. ○
b) When adding more variables to a linear regression model, R^2 cannot decrease. .... ○
c) The model including all 78 available x-variables cannot be estimated by OLS as it is not identified. .... ○
d) Selecting from the 7 candidate models the one with the highest R^2 guarantees the best out-of-sample forecast performance. .... ○

1.3.27. `Single Choice`

You are interested in a linear model that explains monthly wages as the dependent variable y. Based on an extensive review of the literature, you obtained a long list of potential influential factors x_k. Your data set comprises $N = 35$ observations for y and all x_k, $k = 1, \ldots 38$. Which of the following statements regarding model selection is **not** correct?

a) When comparing all potential models in this set-up, in general, the maximum value of R^2 will be close to 1. .... ○
b) Selecting a model, for which BIC is larger than AIC, corresponds to an optimal trade-off between error variance and the number of regressors. .... ○
c) Given a rather low number of observations ($N = 35$), the selection of models based on AIC is recommended. .... ○
d) The model selected by minimizing BIC will, in general, be different from the model obtained by maximizing R^2. .... ○

1.3.28. `Fill-in-the-blank`

Consider a model explaining monthly wages by two dummy variables, `SEX` (= 1 for women) and `FULLTIME` (= 1 for people employed full time). Figure 1.17 provides estimation results for this model based on a sample with $N = 65$ observations.

```
-----------------------------------------------------------
Dependent Variable: WAGE_M        Method: Least Squares
Included observations: 65
-----------------------------------------------------------
Variable       Coeff.      Std. Err.     t-Stat.     Prob.
-----------------------------------------------------------
C             3355.81     555.9412      6.03627     0.0000
SEX          -1041.12     475.7678     -2.18830     0.0324
FULLTIME      928.295     484.0681      1.91770     0.0598
-----------------------------------------------------------
R-squared             0.1993  Mean dependent var 3314.94
Adjusted R-squared 0.1734  S.D. dependent var 1830.15
F-statistic           7.7146  Durbin-Watson stat 2.00470
-----------------------------------------------------------
```

Fig. 1.17. Results of least squares estimation of a wage function.

Please complete the following statement:

The model presented and a model that contains only a constant and the dummy variable SEX are .... in each other. Based on the available information and assuming that all other assumptions for OLS are satisfied, a feasible test for model selection ($\alpha = 0.05$) is the .... Given the result of this test, you would prefer the model .... the FULLTIME dummy.

1.3.29. Single Choice

Consider two models to explain monthly wages. Model A includes the dummy variables SEX (= 1 for women) and FULLTIME (= 1 for people employed full time) as explanatory variables, while Model B comprises the dummy SEX (= 1 for women) and the duration of school education (SCHOOL_T). Which of the following statements regarding the two models is correct?

a) Model A is nested in Model B. .... ○
b) Model B is nested in Model A. .... ○
c) A comparison based on R^2 of both models is not meaningful in this setting. .... ○
d) Choosing the model with lower value of Akaike's information criterion is adequate if the number of observations is rather small. .... ○

1.4 Panel Data

1.4.1. `True or False`

Imagine that you would like to collect data on the management style of 150 firms in each of the years 2025, 2027, and 2029 using an online survey. Your colleague indicates that collecting a panel dataset would be more challenging than collecting cross-sectional datasets for each of the years. Is this statement true or false?

a) True .... ○
b) False .... ○

1.4.2. `Single Choice`

Assume that you want to estimate the effects of factors that influence wages. For this purpose, you have access to a balanced panel of 4 058 individuals from the German Socioeconomic Panel (GSOEP) for the years 2018–2021. Which of the following statements is correct?

a) Using the pooled estimator will take into account individual specific effects implicitly. .... ○
b) The setup would not allow for a fixed effects estimation. .... ○
c) The number of observations is 4 058. .... ○
d) The number of observations is 16 232. .... ○

1.4.3. `True or False`

Assume you want to estimate the effects of factors that influence wages. For this purpose, you have access to a balanced panel of 4 058 individuals from the German Socioeconomic Panel (GSOEP) for the years 2018–2021. In this setting, a pooled estimator is not feasible.

a) True .... ○
b) False .... ○

1.4.4. `Fill-in-the-blank`

Based on the German Socio-Economic Panel (2021), you estimated a pooled regression model for monthly wages as a function of years spent in schooling, age, a dummy for region (East/West Germany), and a dummy for smokers.

Given that the structure of the data has observations for one person over time following each other, you expect that the error terms of the model might exhibit .... To test whether this problem is present, you may consider the ....-statistic, which is often shown as part of the standard output of a linear regression.

1.4.5. `Single Choice`

When working with panel data, individual specific effects are of particular interest. Which of the following statements about individual specific effects is **not** correct?

a) Individual specific effects are only relevant if persons are considered. ○
b) Individual specific effects can be modeled by fixed-effects. .... ○
c) Individual specific effects can be modeled by random-effects only if they are not correlated with other explanatory variables. .... ○
d) Individual specific effects are assumed to be time constant. .... ○

1.4.6. `Single Choice`

Which of the following statements about random- and fixed-effects in a panel regression framework is correct?

a) Fixed effects can be estimated as a function of the explanatory variables in the model. .... ○
b) Random effects are assumed to result from a random drawing from an underlying distribution over the whole population. .... ○
c) Including fixed effects in the model excludes the use of other time-varying regressors. .... ○
d) Including random effects in the model is the better choice if individual specific effects are correlated with other explanatory variables. ...... ○

1.4.7. `Single Choice`

For a model of individual wages (logarithmized) as a function of schooling (`SCHOOLING`), age (`AGE`), age squared (`AGE2`) and a health index (`HEALTH`), panel data are used for estimation. In this context, a text was performed on whether a fixed- or a random-effects model should be used. The following output shows the results of this test:

```
================================================
Test cross-section random effects
================================================
Test Summary              Chi-Sq. Sta  d.f. Prob.
================================================
Cross-section random        142.17       4   0.000
================================================
Cross-section random effects test comparisons:
Variable      Fixed    Random  Var(Diff.)    Prob.
================================================
SCHOOLING      0.0325   0.1060   0.00029     0.0000
AGE            0.0848   0.0658   0.00003     0.0002
AGE2          -0.0005  -0.0006   0.00000     0.1848
HEALTH        -0.0096  -0.0127   0.00000     0.0023
================================================
```

Which of the following statements related to this test is **not** correct?

a) The test summarizes the output of a Wu-Hausmann test with null hypothesis that individual specific effects and explanatory variables are not correlated. .... ○

b) The test statistics is based on a comparison of the estimates from a fixed-effects and a random-effects model. .... ○

b) The value of the test statistics of 142.17 is larger than the 95% percentile of a χ^2-distribution with 4 degrees of freedom. Therefore, the null hypothesis has to be rejected at the 5% level. .... ○

d) Based on the result of the test, the more efficient random-effects estimator should be used. .... ○

1.5 Discrete and Limited Dependent Variables

1.5.1. `Single Choice`

For modeling binary dependent variables, both the Probit and Logit models are often used. Which of the following statements regarding these estimators is correct?

a) The Probit model assumes normally distributed error terms in the equation for the latent variable. .... ○

b) The Logit model assumes log-normal distributed error terms in the equation for the latent variable. .... ○

c) Both models can be estimated by non-linear least squares. .... ○

d) Coefficient estimates of the Logit model are usually smaller (in absolute terms) than those of the Probit model. .... ○

1.5.2. `Single Choice`

For modeling binary dependent variables, the Probit model exhibits some advantages as compared to the linear probability model. Which of the following statements is **not** correct?

a) The Probit model guarantees that forecasted probabilities for outcome 1 are always between 0 and 1 (0% and 100%). .... ○

b) The error terms of the Probit model are homoskedastic. .... ○

c) The coefficients estimated for the Probit model can be interpreted as marginal effects on the probability of obtaining outcome 1. .... ○

d) The Likelihood function for the Probit model corresponds to the probability of observing the outcomes which are actually observed conditional on the model parameters and the values of the explanatory variables. . ○

1.5.3. Single Choice

The following table shows the results of an estimation to explain the employment status of individuals.

```
EMPLOYED     Dummy for having a job (1=Yes, 0=No)
AGE          Age of a person in years
SEX          Dummy for gender (1=female, 0=male)
SCHOOL_T     Number of years spent in school
UNIV         Dummy for university degree (1=Yes, 0=No)

Dependent Variable: EMPLOYED
Method: ML - Binary Probit (Quadratic hill climbing)
Included observations: 1204
Convergence achieved after 4 iterations
======================================================
Variable    Coeff.      Std. Error   z-Stat.     Prob.
======================================================
C            3.5781      0.5684      6.2950     0.0000
AGE         -0.0543      0.0024    -22.625      0.0000
SEX         -0.4612      0.0391    -11.795      0.0000
SCHOOL_T     0.7177      0.0091     78.868      0.0000
UNIV         0.3149      0.0494      6.3745     0.0000
======================================================
McFadden R-squared     0.4691  Mean depend. var   0.8764
S.D. dependent var     0.4286  S.E. of regres.    0.2741
Akaike info criterion  0.9232  Sum squared resid 1967.7
Schwarz criterion      0.9315  Log likelihood   -3173.3
Hannan-Quinn criter.   0.9311  Restr. log like. -5977.1
LR statistic           5607.5  Prob(LR stat.)     0.0000
======================================================
```

Which of the following statements is **not** correct based on the above output?

a) Having obtained a university degree increases the probability of being employed significantly (at the 5%-level). .... ○

b) The marginal effect of one more year of schooling on the probability of being employed cannot be read off from the output. .... ○

c) The null hypothesis that all explanatory variables jointly have no impact on the probability of being employed can be rejected at the 5%-level based on the LR statistic. .... ○

d) The employment probability of females is about 46 percentage points lower than for males. .... ○

1.5.4. Single Choice

The following table shows the results of an estimation to explain whether a firm survives a business year ($y_i = 1$) or not ($y_i = 0$) based on 1254 observations for German firms and the business year 2023. The second explanatory variable (X2) is a measure of the firm's debt ratio at the beginning of the business year (i.e. total debt divided by total assets).

```
Dependent Variable: Y
Method: ML - Binary Probit (Quadratic hill climbing)
Included observations: 1254
Convergence achieved after 5 iterations
Covariance matrix computed using second derivatives
======================================================
Variable    Coeff.      Std. Error    z-Stat.      Prob.
======================================================
Const         2.9474       0.2683      10.9837     0.0000
X1            1.9799       0.1698      11.6587     0.0000
X2           -0.9845       0.0855     -11.5137     0.0000
X3            0.5556       0.0541      10.2656     0.0000
======================================================
McFadden R-squared    0.7547  Mean depend. var    0.7850
S.D. dependent var    0.4110  S.E. of regres.     0.2004
Akaike info crit.     0.2634  Sum squared resid  39.998
Schwarz criterion     0.2830  Log likelihood    -127.70
Hannan-Quinn criter. 0.2709  Restr.log like.   -520.51
LR statistic          785.61  Prob(LR stat.)      0.0000
======================================================
```

Which of the following statements is **not** correct based on the above output?

a) It is possible to conclude that a higher value of the debt ratio (X2) decreases the probability of surviving the business year. .... ○

b) The marginal effect of an increase in the debt ratio by 1 percentage point is -0.98%. .... ○

c) The effect of an increase in the debt ratio is significantly different from 0 at the 5% level assuming that all assumptions for the model are satisfied. .... ○

d) The null hypothesis that all explanatory variables jointly have no effect on the probability of surviving the business year can be rejected at the 1% level based on the LR statistic shown in the output. .... ○

1.5.5. Single Choice

The following table shows the results of an estimation to model the highest school leaving degree (SCHOOL) obtained by individuals.

```
SCHOOL:     (1 - 4 corresponding to 9,10,12 and 13 years
             of schooling)
AGE:        Age of a person in years
SEX:        Dummy for gender (1=female, 0=male)
MIGBACK:    Dummy for migration background (1=yes, 0=no)

Dependent Variable: SCHOOL
Method: ML - Ordered Probit  (Newton-Raphson...)
Included observations: 14732
Convergence achieved after 7 iterations
Coeff. covariance computed using observed Hessian
```

Variable	Coeff.	Std. Error	z-Stat.	Prob.
AGE	-0.0160	0.0005	-29.3573	0.0000
SEX	-0.0923	0.0458	-2.0168	0.0437
MIGBACK	-0.1560	0.0264	-6.0497	0.0000
SEX*MIGBACK	0.0778	0.0355	2.1914	0.0284

Which of the following statements is **not** correct based on the above output?

a) For a woman without migration background the probability of having obtained the highest school leaving degree (SCHOOL = 4) is about 9,23% lower as compared to men without migration background of same age. ○

b) For older people it is less likely to have obtained the highest shool leaving degree (SCHOOL = 4) ceteris paribus. . . . . ○

c) The effect of a migration background is significantly different from zero for men. . . . . ○

d) Without further calculations it is not possible to judge whether higher age increases the probability of a person to have SCHOOL = 2 rather than SCHOOL = 3. . . . . ○

1.5.6. Single Choice

Table 1.1 shows the results of the estimation of a multinomial Logit model to explain the marital status of 9,444 individuals of the German Socio-Economic Panel 2021 who are either married (1), single, i.e., never married (2), divorced (3) or widowed (4). The explanatory factors are the individual monthly gross wage in 1 000 Euro (WAGE) and age (AGE). The “married” category was chosen as the reference category.

	single	divorced	widowed
CONST	2.9684	-3.5886	-9.3758
	(0.1193)	(0.2102)	(0.5655)
WAGE	-0.0064	-0.1040	-0.2028
	(0.0165)	(0.0208)	(0.0469)
AGE	-0.0913	0.0430	0.1190
	(0.0026)	(0.0040)	(0.0098)

Table 1.1. Results of the multinomial Logit model (standard errors in parentheses).

Which of the following statements **cannot** be supported by the estimates assuming that all required assumptions for the econometric model are satisfied?

a) Increasing AGE makes it ceteris paribus less likely to be a single as compared to be married. .... ○

b) The effect of WAGE on the probability of being widowed rather than married is significantly different from zero. .... ○

c) The effect of WAGE on the probability of single rather than married is significantly different from zero. .... ○

d) Without further calculations it is not possible to judge by how much an increase of wages by 1,000 Euro, i.e., an increase of WAGE by one, would decrease the probability of being a single as compared to be married. ○

2

Open Exercises

2.0 Matrix Algebra and Principles of Inferential Statistics

Matrix Algebra

2.0.1. Let λ be a scalar, x be a column vector of length N, $\mathbf{A}$ a matrix of dimension $N \times K$, and $\mathbf{B}$ a matrix of dimension $K \times N$, where N and K can be any positive integer number, i.e., $N, K \in \mathbb{N}^+$. Indicate under which conditions on N and K the following operations are admitted.

a) λx

b) $\mathbf{A} + \mathbf{B}$

c) $\lambda \mathbf{A}$

d) $\mathbf{A}\mathbf{A}'x$

e) $\mathbf{B}\mathbf{B}'x$

2.0.2. Consider the following matrices:

$$A = \begin{pmatrix} 11 & 8 & 7 \\ -3 & -2 & 5 \\ 18 & -10 & 7 \end{pmatrix}, \quad B = \begin{pmatrix} 15 & 0 & 2 & -6 \\ 5 & 3 & 8 & 2 \\ 8 & 4 & 5 & -2 \end{pmatrix}, \quad C = \begin{pmatrix} 2 & 0 & 0 \\ 0 & 1 & 1 \\ 2 & 1 & 1 \end{pmatrix}$$

Determine the rank and trace of the matrices if these concepts are defined.

2.0.3. When dealing with the linear regression model, the matrix

$$M = (I - X(X'X)^{-1}X')$$

is relevant. It is also called the residual maker matrix. Assume that X is an $N \times K$ matrix of full rank and I is the $N \times N$ identity matrix with ones on the diagonal and zeros elsewhere. Demonstrate that M is an idempotent matrix.

P. Winker, *Exercise Book Advanced Econometrics*,
https://doi.org/10.1007/978-3-662-74252-5_2

Principles of Inferential Statistics

2.0.4. Explain the law of large numbers.

2.0.5. Sketch a proof of the central theorem of statistics based on the law of large numbers.

2.0.6. Consider independently distributed random numbers $X_i \sim N(0, 1)$ (standard normal distribution), for $i = 1, \ldots, \infty$ and $Y_i \sim U([0, 1)]$ (uniform distribution on $[0, 1]$), for $i = 1, \ldots, \infty$. Describe the (approximate) form of the density function of the random numbers described by the following functionals and provide an argument for your choice.

a) $X_1 + X_2$

b) $Y_1 + Y_2$

c) $Y_1^2 + Y_2^2 + \ldots Y_n^2$ for $n \longrightarrow \infty$

d) $X_1^2 + X_2^2 + X_3^2 + X_4^2$

2.0.7. You have a random sample of drawings $x_1, \ldots, x_n$ from a normal distribution $N(\mu, \sigma^2)$.

a) Describe the construction of a 95% confidence interval for μ based on the mean of the sample $\bar{x} = \frac{1}{n}\sum_{i=1}^{n} x_i$ and the variance of the sample $\hat{\sigma}^2 = \frac{1}{n-1}\sum_{i=1}^{n}\left(x_i^2 - \bar{x}^2\right)^2$.

b) How would the interval change when fixing a 99% confidence level? What would be the expected change of the interval if μ increases? What would be the expected change of the interval if σ decreases?

c) Describe the construction of a 95% confidence interval for σ^2 based on the sample.

d) Describe the procedure to test whether $\mu = 0$, based on the random sample. Start by formulating the null hypothesis. What test statistic would you use? Derive the distribution of this test statistic under the null hypothesis, i.e., when $\mu = 0$ actually holds. Finally, explain when the null hypothesis must be rejected when allowing for a maximum probability of an error of type 1 of 5%.

2.1 Approach and Principles of Econometric Modeling

The Role of Econometrics

2.1.1. Use an example of your choice to explain the steps leading from the observation of economic phenomena to hypotheses which might be tested by means of econometric methods.

2.1.2. Discuss an example of an application of econometric methods with a focus on the quantification of one or more parameters of interest. In particular, you should highlight why knowledge about the value(s) of the parameter(s) is relevant.

2.1.3. Describe an example in which the testing of a hypothesis regarding an economic model is relevant.

2.1.4. List the three central ingredients of the econometric analysis and explain their relevance for the outcome of the analysis.

2.1.5. Explain the difference between reduced form and structural models using an example of your choice. No formal derivation is required.

2.1.6. Consider the simplified macroeconomic model of a closed economy

$$\begin{aligned} C_t &= \beta_0 + \beta_1 Y_t + \beta_2 r_t + \varepsilon_{C,t} \\ I_t &= \gamma_0 + \gamma_1 r_t + \varepsilon_{I,t} \\ Y_t &= C_t + I_t + G_t , \end{aligned}$$

where C_t denotes private consumption, I_t investment, and Y_t output in period t, which are assumed to be endogenous. The interest rate r_t and the public expenditure G_t is assumed to be given exogenously. ε_{C_t} and $\varepsilon_{I,t}$ are assumed to be normally distributed exogenous shocks with expected value zero and variance $\sigma^2_{\varepsilon C}$ and $\sigma^2_{\varepsilon_I}$, respectively.

a) List all parameters of this structural model?

b) Derive a reduced form model, i.e., a representation of the model, where endogenous variables only show up on the left hand side of the equations.

c) List all parameters of the reduced form model?

d) Is it possible to obtain estimates of some or all structural parameters based on estimates for the reduced form model?

What is Special about Microeconomic Data?

2.1.7. Consider the model $y_i = \beta_1 + \beta_2 x_i + u_i$, where the x_i are sampled from a normal distribution with expected value 20 and a variance of 25, while u_i are also normally distributed with expected value zero and a variance of one. The coefficients β_1 and β_2 are set to 1 and 0.9, respectively. Based on a random sample of size 100, the estimates $\hat{\beta}_1$ and $\hat{\beta}_2$ are 1.1701 and 0.8969, i.e., quite close to their actual values in the population. Figure 7 shows a scatter plot of the data in the right panel (A).

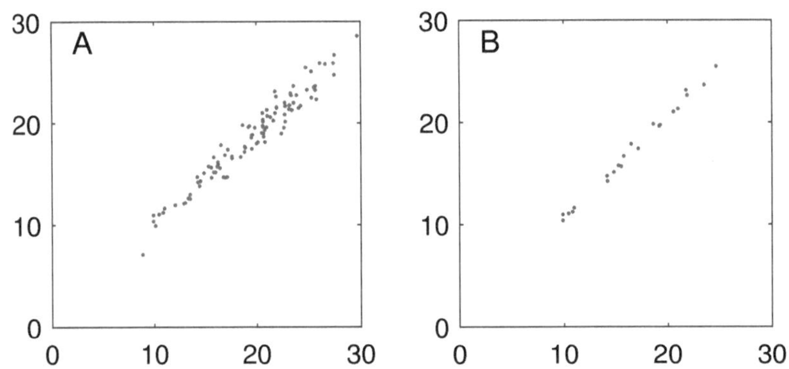

Using 1.000 random subsets of size 20, 95% of the estimates $\hat{\beta}_2$ fall in the interval $[0,8075, 0.973]$.

The left panel of the figure (B) shows the subset of data obtained by imposing the condition $y_i > x_i$, which comprises 20 observations. Estimating the model based on this subset results in an estimator $\hat{\beta}_2 = 1.004$.

Use this example to explain the issue of *sample selection* in econometric applications. In particular, address the risk of biased estimates due to non-random sample selection.

2.1.8. You are going to study the impact of wage rates on individual labor supply. Therefore, you study the relationship $H_i = f(W_i) + u_i$, where H_i stands for the hours worked per week, W_i for the hourly wage rate, and u_i for an additive error term of the person i. When drafting the unknown function in a scatter diagram of W and H, one might see a non-linear relationship. Explain why this function is likely to exhibit a kink (starting flat and then starting to increase) or a jump with a kink (starting flat and then jumping to a positive value and increasing steadily afterwards).

2.1.9. Consider a standard linear regression model $Y_i = \beta_1 + \beta_2 X_i + u_i$, Describe the property of exogeneity of X in this model formally and intuitively. Provide an example of such a relationship, when the assumption of exogeneity of X is likely to hold, and another one, when it is likely to fail.

2.2 Estimation

Ordinary Least Squares

2.2.1 Please provide a formal proof that for given **X** the least squares estimator satisfies the property U from BLUE. To simplify the notation, you can use the compact matrix notation for the model, i.e., $Y = X\beta + u$.

2.2.2. For the proof of 2.2.1, you did not have to use the assumptions $u \overset{iid}{\sim} N(0, \sigma_u^2)$. Indicate shortly which assumptions the notation $u \overset{iid}{\sim} N(0, \sigma_u^2)$ summarizes. Explain for one of these assumptions how it may affect estimates of the coefficients or of the variance of coefficients.

Nonlinear Least Squares

2.2.3. You are interested in estimating the parameters of a Cobb-Douglas production function for an aggregate economy. You have data for the variables real output (Y_t), real capital stock (K_t) and employment L_t and want to estimate the parameters α and β of the model

$$Y_t = AK_t^{\alpha} L_t^{\beta} u_t ,$$

where the constant A is a measure of technology and u_t are assumed to be error factors with values around one.

a) Describe how you can estimate these parameters using OLS making use of the natural logarithm.

b) Provide at least one argument in favor of using this approach rather than applying NLS to the original non-linear model.

2.2.4. You estimate the classical aggregate Cobb-Douglas production function for Germany with time series data for 1991 to 2024 for GDP (Y), capital (K) and labor (tt L) and obtain the following results.

```
=====================================================
Dependent Variable: Y
Method: Least Squares (Gauss-Newton/Marquardt steps)
Sample: 1991 2025            Included observations: 35
Y=EXP(C(1))*K^C(2)*L^C(3)
=====================================================
         Coefficient   Std. Error   t-Statistic   Prob.
=====================================================
C(1)      -3.579331     0.242326    -14.77074    0.0000
C(2)       0.710562     0.068308     10.40230    0.0000
C(3)       0.842881     0.099695     8.454595    0.0000
=====================================================
```

a) Write down the estimated model in the usual notation using u_t for the error term in period t. Note that coefficients are labeled in EViews as `C(1)`, `C(2))`, and `C(3)`. The estimated relationship is shown on line 4 of the output.

b) Provide an interpretation of the coefficients `C(2)` and `C(3)`. Are they statistically significant different from zero?

2.2.5. You estimate the classical aggregate Cobb-Douglas production function for Germany with time series data for 1991 to 2024 for GDP (`Y`) capital (`K`) and labor (`L`) and obtain the following results. Note that coefficients are labeled in EViews as `C(1)`, `C(2))`, and `C(3)`. The estimated relationship is shown on line 5 of the output.

```
=====================================================
Dependent Variable: Y
Method: Least Squares (Gauss-Newton/Marquardt steps)
Sample: 1991 2025          Included observations: 35
Failure to improve ssr (...) after 1 iteration
Y=EXP(C(1))*K^C(2)*L^C(3)
=====================================================
       Coefficient   Std. Error  t-Statistic   Prob.
=====================================================
C(1)    -18.47975    617.765296   -0.02991   0.97632
C(2)    3.4508736    259.688525    0.01329   0.98948
C(3)    2.2481808    303.693303    0.00740   0.99414
=====================================================
```

a) According to the results presented, are the coefficients `C(2)` and `C(3)` statistically significant different from zero?

b) Are the estimated values for coefficients `C(2)` and `C(3)` plausible from an economic point of view?

c) What information provided in the output points to some numerical issues with the estimate?

Generalized Least Squares

2.2.6. Consider the linear regression model

$$\boldsymbol{y} = \boldsymbol{X}\boldsymbol{\beta} + \boldsymbol{u} \quad , \tag{2.1}$$

where $\boldsymbol{y}$ and $\boldsymbol{u}$ are of dimension $n \times 1$ and $\boldsymbol{X}$ is an $n \times k$ matrix. Let $\boldsymbol{\Omega} = E(\boldsymbol{u}\boldsymbol{u}')$ denote the covariance matrix of the independently normally distributed error terms, which is known to be a diagonal matrix containing n different non-zero elements. Furthermore, it is assumed that $E(\boldsymbol{X}'\boldsymbol{u}) = \boldsymbol{0}$ holds.

a) Is the OLS estimator $\hat{\beta} = \left(\boldsymbol{X}'\boldsymbol{X}\right)^{-1}\boldsymbol{X}'\boldsymbol{y}$ efficient in this setting? Please also derive the variance of the OLS estimator when applied in this setting.

b) If all elements in $\boldsymbol{\Omega}$ are known, its inverse can be factorized through a unique Cholesky decomposition into $\boldsymbol{\Omega}^{-1} = \boldsymbol{P}'\boldsymbol{P}$. Now assume that the linear model given above is transformed into a new model by pre-multiplying it with the matrix $\boldsymbol{P}$, i.e.

$$\underbrace{\boldsymbol{Py}}_{\boldsymbol{y}^*} = \underbrace{\boldsymbol{PX}}_{\boldsymbol{X}^*}\beta + \underbrace{\boldsymbol{Pu}}_{\boldsymbol{u}^*}, \tag{2.2}$$

and the unknown coefficients β of this new model are estimated using the OLS method.

Why can the OLS regression of this model also be seen as a special type of "generalized least squares (GLS)" regression of the original model called "weighted least squares"? What are the weights, which of the n observations receive a high weight?

c) Derive the variance of the new error vector $\boldsymbol{u}^*$. What does the result imply for the efficiency of the OLS estimator applied to the transformed model?

d) The following figure shows a scatter plot of $n = 8$ observation pairs (y_i, x_i) and a linear fit whose parameters were estimated by regressing y_i on a constant and the one independent variable x_i (so $k = 2$ holds) employing the OLS method.

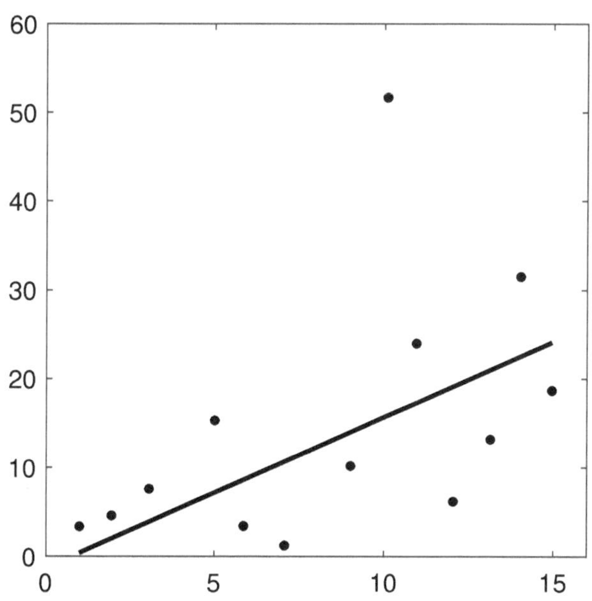

Assume that the correct model specification has been chosen. When the observations y_i are uncorrelated but can only be measured with different known uncertainties – in particular the uncertainty is linearly increasing in the value of x_i – what will the regression line look like if GLS instead of OLS is applied as the estimation method? Draw an approximate GLS regression line in the figure in addition to the OLS line already depicted and explain what causes differences between both lines (if there are any)!

e) The estimation of the original model by GLS is a rather theoretical procedure which is practically not feasible since the elements of the diagonal matrix $\boldsymbol{\Omega}$ are typically not directly observable. Explain how an estimate $\hat{\boldsymbol{\Omega}}$ can be derived and thus GLS can be rendered feasible if one knows that the variance of each observation i is dependent on one of the regressors, denoted $x_{1,i}$, through the relationship

$$Var(u_i) = \gamma_0 + \gamma_1 x_{1,i}\,, \forall\, i = 1, 2, \ldots, n\,. \tag{2.3}$$

2.2.7. Consider the linear regression model

$$\boldsymbol{y} = \boldsymbol{X}\boldsymbol{\beta} + \boldsymbol{u} \quad , \tag{2.4}$$

where $\boldsymbol{y}$ and $\boldsymbol{u}$ are of dimension $n \times 1$ and $\boldsymbol{X}$ is an $n \times k$ matrix. Let $\boldsymbol{\Omega} = E(\boldsymbol{u}\boldsymbol{u}')$ denote the covariance matrix of the independently normally distributed error terms, which is known to be a diagonal matrix with identical values of the non-zero elements. It is assumed that $E(\boldsymbol{X}'\boldsymbol{u}) = \mathbf{0}$ does **not** hold.

a) Describe shortly the central idea of using *instruments* in this context. What are the main assumptions for good instruments?

b) Which two estimation procedures could be applied using instruments?

2.2.8. Consider the following output of a model estimated to explain the monthly wage (WAGE_M in Euro) of 1,546 employed persons in 2012. The data are taken from the German Socio-Economic Panel. The explanatory variables are the following:

SCHOOL_T	Time spent in schooling (years)
EDU_FATHER	Highest educational degree of father (scale: 1 - 3)
EDU_MOTHER	Highest educational degree of mother (scale: 1 - 3)

```
=====================================================
Dependent Variable: WAGE_M
Method: Two-Stage Least Squares
Included observations: 1546
Instrument specification:
        (EDU_FATHER = 2) (EDU_FATHER = 3)
        (EDU_MOTHER = 2) (EDU_MOTHER = 3) C
=====================================================
```

Variable	Coefficient	Std. Error	t-Statistic	Prob.
C	162.2791	1089.919	0.148891	0.8817
SCHOOL_T	295.9228	101.5414	2.914307	0.0036
R-squared	0.16153	Mean dependent var	3336.845	

a) What was the average monthly wage of the persons in the sample?

b) Which model type was estimated? What could have been a reason to choose this model type?

c) Does the provided output allow judging whether the chosen model is appropriate?

d) Assuming that all required assumptions for the model are met, how large is the effect of one additional year of schooling? Is this effect statistically significant different from zero?

Maximum Likelihood

2.2.9. Describe shortly the difference between the least squares and the maximum likelihood estimation with respect to the objective function to be optimized.

2.2.10. Consider the linear regression model

$$\boldsymbol{y} = \boldsymbol{X}\boldsymbol{\beta} + \boldsymbol{u} \quad , \tag{2.5}$$

where $\boldsymbol{y}$ and $\boldsymbol{u}$ are of dimension $n \times 1$ and $\boldsymbol{X}$ is an $n \times k$ matrix. Let $\boldsymbol{\Omega} = E(\boldsymbol{u}\boldsymbol{u}')$ denote the covariance matrix of the independently normally distributed error terms, which is known to be a diagonal matrix. Furthermore, for a variable $\boldsymbol{z}$ that might be part of $\boldsymbol{X}$ or not, but is observed in any case, it holds that the $var(u_i) = \alpha_1 + \alpha_2 z_i + \alpha_3 z_i^2$, i.e., the error terms are not homoscedastic. Finally, it is assumed that $E(\boldsymbol{X}'\boldsymbol{u}) = \boldsymbol{0}$.

a) Derive the log-likelihood function for this model.

b) Are the estimates of α_1, α_2 and α_3 that would result from maximizing this log-likelihood function consistent?

c) Describe an estimator of the asymptotic variance of ML-estimators.

Generalized Method of Moments

2.2.11. Explain the idea of GMM and approach when there are more moment restrictions than parameters. Why is this setting of overidentification welcome?

2.2.12. Consider the linear regression model

$$y = X\beta + u \quad , \tag{2.6}$$

where y and u are of dimension $n\times 1$ and X is an $n\times k$ matrix. Let $\Omega = E(uu')$ denote the covariance matrix of the independently normally distributed error terms, which is known to be a diagonal matrix with equal entries on the diagonal (homoscedastic). Given that it is assumed that $E(X'u) \neq 0$, a set of $l > k$ instruments Z that satisfies $E(Z'u) \neq 0$ is used.

a) Describe the moment conditions used for the instrumental variable estimator using GMM.

b) How many moment restrictions are there for the specified setting?

c) Derive the GMM estimator of β assuming that $\frac{\hat{\sigma}^2}{N}Z'Z$ is a consistent estimator of $var(\frac{1}{N}Z'u)$. How does this estimator differ from the 2SLS estimator?

2.2.13. Shortly explain one advantage of GMM estimation compared to ML estimation.

2.3 Hypothesis Testing and Model Selection

Linear Hypothesis

2.3.1. Consider the following linear model:

$$Y_t = \beta_0 + \beta_1 X_{1,t} + \beta_2 X_{2,t} + \ldots + \beta_k X_{k,t} + u_t \, , t = 1, ..., 21$$

a) First, we assume that all relevant assumptions about the model are satisfied. Then, we would like to test the following hypotheses:
H_0^1: $\beta_2 = 1$
H_0^2: $\beta_1/\beta_2 = 2$
H_0^3: $\beta_1\beta_2 = 0.5$
H_0^4: $\beta_1 = \beta_2 = \ldots = \beta_k = 0$
Which of these hypotheses can be analyzed making use of standard t- or F-tests (i.e. tests for linear hypothesis)?

b) For one of the hypotheses shown above, provide R and r for the general test of linear hypotheses $R\beta - r = 0$.

2.3.2. Assume that all model assumptions are satisfied for both the OLS estimator and the ML estimator of a linear model, respectively. The distribution of error terms in the ML setting does not have to be a normal one. In this setting, what is the difference regarding the interpretation of t-statistics (for testing linear hypothesis about one parameter) between OLS and ML?

General Hypothesis

2.3.3. For a linear regression model, the least squares estimator and the maximum likelihood estimator are identical under the assumption of independently, identically normally distributed error terms. Thus, the testing methodology of the maximum likelihood framework can also be applied for testing nonlinear hypotheses about the parameters of the model.

a) Describe the basic ideas of the Wald- and the LM-test in the maximum likelihood setting, possibly making use of a graphical presentation.

b) Although both tests provide the same results asymptotically, for specific purposes one or the other of the two tests is preferable for practical reasons. Describe one setting in which either the Wald- or the LM-test is preferable and explain why.

2.3.4. A linear hypothesis in a linear regression model could be tested by the Wald-test or the F-test.

a) Under which condition would you prefer the F-test based on the F-statistic?

b) What would be the advantage of using the F-test under this condition?

2.3.5. Figure 5 shows the stylized course of a log-likelihood function $lnL(\theta)$ (solid line, left axis) and of a (nonlinear) restriction function $c(\theta)$ (dotted line,right axis) as a function of a scalar parameter θ. The dotted horizontal line is the zero line for the right axis, i.e., relevant for $c(\theta)$, while all values of $lnL(\theta)$ are smaller than or equal to zero (left axis).

a) Use the figure to provide an intuitive description of the idea of the LR-test and the Wald-test of hypothesis $c(\theta) = 0$, where c denotes the constraint function (it is required but not sufficient to add elements to the figure).

b) When would you prefer to use the Wald-test compared to the LR-test to test $H_0 : c(\theta) = 0$?

2.3.6. Please consider the following output of a test regarding the assumptions of a linear regression model for explaining housing expenditures `RENT`, when answering the further questions below. The explanatory variables are the following:

`WAGE`	Monthly wage (gross)
`NO_CHILD`	Number of children
`DSMOKER`	Dummy for paying smoker (= 1 yes, = 0 no)

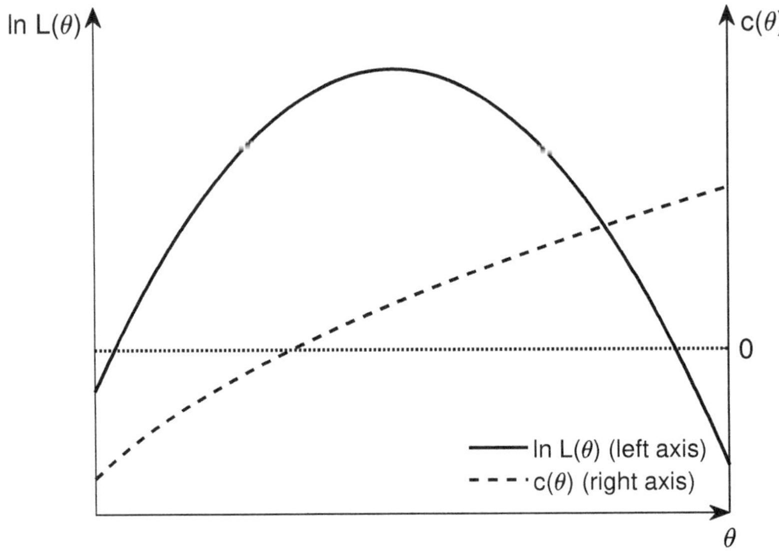

Fig. 2.1. Stylized log-likelihood function and restriction function.

```
===========================================================
Test:
Null hypothesis:
===========================================================
F-statistic       3.9488     Prob. F(8,3051)        0.0001
Obs*R-squared    31.3586     Prob. Chi-Square(8)    0.0001
===========================================================
```

```
===========================================================
Test Equation:      Dependent Variable: RESID^2
Method: Least Squares      Included observations: 3060
Collinear test regressors dropped from specification
===========================================================
Variable             Coeff.   Std.Err  t-Statistic  Prob.
===========================================================
C                   5240290   614528    8.52734     0.0000
WAGE^2             -0.03554   0.0293   -1.21222     0.2255
WAGE*NO_CHILD       91.2935   64.348    1.41875     0.1561
WAGE*DSMOKER        110.868   195.25    0.56782     0.5702
WAGE                501.341   279.33    1.79484     0.0728
NO_CHILD^2          79254.5   114833    0.69017     0.4901
NO_CHILD*DSMOKER  -123198.    334740   -0.36804     0.7129
NO_CHILD          -119653.    414552   -0.28863     0.7729
DSMOKER^2         -330135.    764455   -0.43186     0.6659
===========================================================
R-squared   0.010248    Mean dependent var 6760998.33
===========================================================
```

a) Which assumption of the linear regression model was tested? What is the Null hypothesis of the test. How is the test named?

b) Which conclusion can be drawn from the output with respect to the null hypothesis formulated in a)? Which value(s) in the output do you use to determine that?

c) What does the statement in the output "`Colinear test regressors dropped from specification`" mean? Which variable(s) should have been included additionally normally for the test? Why is it/are they dropped?

d) Write down the underlying estimated linear model, for which this test was conducted. Label the variables according to the output (the dependent variable is $\texttt{RENT}_i$) and the cofficients as $\beta_0, \beta_1, \ldots$.

2.3.7. The following table shows the results of an estimation using data from from the German Socioeconomic Panel (GSOEP) for the year 2010. The variable list includes:

DRENT	Dummy for paying rent for housing (= 1 yes, = 0 no, i.e. owning house/appartment)
WAGE	Monthly wage (gross)
NO_CHILDREN	Number of children

```
Dependent Variable: DRENT
Method: ML - Binary Probit (Quadratic hill climbing)
Included observations: 3615
Convergence achieved after 4 iterations
=====================================================
Variable     Coefficient Std. Error    z-Stat.    Prob.
=====================================================
C               0.048891    0.052766   0.926560  0.3542
WAGE           -4.97E-05    1.37E-05  -3.621700  0.0003
NO_CHILDREN -0.177614    0.020914  -8.492685  0.0000
=====================================================
McFadden R-squared  0.0159  Mean dependent var 0.3687
S.D. dependent var  0.4825  S.E. of regression 0.4771
Akaike info crit.   1.2972  Sum squared resid  822.35
Schwarz criterion   1.3024  Log likelihood    -2341.7
Hannan-Quinn crit.  1.2991  Restr. log likel. -2379.7
LR statistic       75.9066  Prob(LR statistic) 0.0000
=====================================================
```

a) Based on the results presented above, is it possible to decide whether the gross wage income increases or decreases significantly (at 5% level) the probability of living in a rented house/apartment? Please explain shortly.

b) From the estimation output above you can also read off the value for `LR statistic` of 75.9066. Please explain how it is obtained from the two reported values for `Log likelihood` and `Restr. log likel.` and what these two values stand for. Which conclusion can be derived based on the reported value of the `LR statistic`?

Hypothesis about Model Assumptions

2.3.8. Based on the German Socio-Economic Panel (2021), you estimated a linear regression model for rent payments as a function of monthly wages, number of children in the household, region (East/West Germany), and a dummy for smokers. You are concerned that the functional form chosen (linear) is not correct and want to run a test.

a) Which test can be used to test the H_0: functional form is correct? Please provide the name of the test and the general idea – no formal presentation is required.

b) The following output shows parts of the results of running the test for the rent payment equation:

```
XXXXXX YYYYYY Test
Omitted Variables: Squares of fitted values
Specification: RENT C WAGE_M NR_CHILD DEAST DSMOKER
===================================================
                   Value        df        Probability
F-statistic       2.5553    (1, 3054)        0.1100
===================================================
```

Based on these results, would you have to reject the null hypothesis of correct functional form at the 5% level? Please shortly explain your answer. Would you therefore stick to the original linear model?

2.3.9. Describe two methods that can be used to test the assumption of no autocorrelation of error terms based on the residuals of a linear regression model. Indicate advantages and disadvantages of both methods in specific settings.

2.3.10. Assume that a colleague of yours would like to estimate a wage regression with observations (individuals) taken from the German Socioeconomic Panel (GSOEP) 2021. She specifies the following linear model and **believes** that the error term is well behaved, in particular, that $u_i \overset{iid}{\sim} N(0, \sigma_u^2 I)$ in the regression model

$$\text{WAGE\_M}_i = \beta_0 + \beta_1\ \text{SCHOOL\_T}_i + \beta_2\ \text{AGE}_i + \beta_3\ \text{SEX}_i + \beta_4\ \text{DEAST}_i + u_i\ ,$$

where the variables are given by:

`WAGE_M:   monthly gross wage of full time`

```
            employed individuals
SCHOOL_T:   years of schooling
AGE:        age in years
SEX:        dummy variable (1 = woman)
DEAST:      dummy variable (1 = living in East Germany)
```

a) Shortly state what heteroskedasticity means in general and provide an economic explanation of why the present model might suffer from heteroskedasticity. Would heteroskedasticity lead to an inconsistent estimation of the parameters?

b) The following EViews output shows the results of an application of the `White test` to the estimated model.

```
Heteroskedasticity Test: White
Null hypothesis: Homoskedasticity
======================================================
F-statistic    0.711522  Prob. F(16,6415)      0.7850
Obs*R-squared 11.39429   Prob. Chi-Square(16)  0.7845
======================================================
```

- Provide the null hypothesis and explain the idea and, accordingly, the testing procedure.
- For the present application, was the `White test` performed with or without cross products? Explain your answer briefly.
- What conclusions would you draw about H_0 for this specific application?

2.3.11. Describe a procedure for testing the null hypothesis that the error terms of a linear regression model are normally distributed. Explain the test statistic and which values are expected for it when the null hypothesis holds true. Also indicate the critical value at the 5% level for rejecting the null hypothesis.

2.3.12. The following EViews output shows some results of estimating a consumption function with private consumption (`PRIV_CONS`) as dependent and disposable income (`DISP_INC`) as explanatory variable based on German quarterly data for the period 1991 to 2025 in billions of euros.

```
Dependent Variable: PRIV_CONS    Method: Least Squares
Sample: 1991Q1 2025Q4        Included observations: 140
======================================================
Variable  Coefficient Std. Error  t-Statistic    Prob.
======================================================
C          -1.44760     3.71493    -0.38967     0.6974
DISP_INC    0.89375     0.00868    102.947      0.0000
======================================================
R-squared          0.98715  Mean dependent var  368.790
F-statistic        10598.1  Durbin-Watson stat  1.48924
======================================================
```

a) Is it possible to make a statement on the mean of private consumption over the period considered just based on the output provided? If yes, please provide the value, otherwise give a short explanation why it is not possible.

b) For which of the standard assumptions regarding the error terms of a linear model does the output provide a test statistic? What is the null hypothesis of this test? Has the null hypothesis to be rejected?

c) Assuming that the null hypothesis of the test has to be rejected, what would be the implication of the interpretation of the size and significance of the coefficient of DISP_INC?

d) Still assuming that the null hypothesis of test in b) has to be rejected, what could be a possible reason for this and how could the model be modified to avoid the problem?

2.3.13. You run a linear regression model for the gross monthly wages of 7,925 German employees in 2023. The explanatory variables include highest shool leaving degree, age, and gender. You run some tests concerning the error terms and, among others, obtain a value of the Jarque-Bera statistic of 16,411,644.

a) Which property of the error terms is tested using the Jarque-Bera statistic? Indicate the null hypothesis of the test and whether it has to be rejected or not at the 5% level.

b) Assuming that the null hypothesis in a) had to be rejected, how would this affect the interpretation of coefficient estimates or t-statistics related to individual coefficients?

c) Is a rejection of the null hypothesis of major relevance in the presented setting? Shortly explain your argument.

Model Selection

2.3.14. You are interested in a linear model that explains monthly wages as the dependent variable y. Based on an extensive review of the literature, you obtained a long list of potential influential factors x_k. Your data set comprises $N = 65$ observations for y and all x_k, $k = 1, \ldots 78$.

In a first attempt to find a good model, you compare 7 models comprising between 2 and 16 different explanatory variables. One of your colleagues suggested using the R^2 of the models considered for model selection.

a) Describe shortly what R^2 measures for a linear model. When following your colleague's advice, which of the 7 models would you choose?

b) What problem is related to the use of R^2 for model selection in this context?

c) An alternative way to select the best out of the 7 models is given by information criteria. Explain the principle of what these criteria measure. Which of the criteria would you use in the present setup – provide a brief explanation. Which model would you choose based on the values of your preferred information criterion?

2.3.15. You are interested in a linear model that explains monthly wages as the dependent variable y. Based on an extensive review of the literature, you obtained a long list of potential influential factors x_k. Your data set comprises $N = 65$ observations for y and all x_k, $k = 1, \ldots 78$.

Based on some preliminary analyses, you decide to start with a model containing only the dummies `SEX` (= 1 for women) and `FULLTIME` (= 1 for people employed full time) (Model 1) or `SEX` and years spent in education `SCHOOL_T` (Model 2), respectively. The following outputs provide results for these models:

Model 1:

```
Dependent Variable: WAGE_M        Method: Least Squares
Included observations: 65
=======================================================
Variable  Coefficient  Std. Error  t-Statistic   Prob.
=======================================================
C            3355.809    555.9412     6.036265  0.0000
SEX         -1041.124    475.7678    -2.188302  0.0324
FULLTIME     928.2950    484.0681     1.917695  0.0598
=======================================================
R-squared            0.1993   Mean dependent var 3314.9
S.E. of regression   1663.9   Akaike info crit.  17.717
Sum squared resid    2E+08    Schwarz criterion  17.817
F-statistic          7.7146   Durbin-Watson stat 2.0047
=======================================================
```

Model 2:

```
Dependent Variable: WAGE_M        Method: Least Squares
Included observations: 65
=======================================================
Variable  Coefficient  Std. Error  t-Statistic   Prob.
=======================================================
C             2004.458   725.5993     2.762486  0.0075
SEX          -1451.046   401.3283    -3.615609  0.0006
SCHOOL_T      211.2435   62.61895     3.373475  0.0013
=======================================================
R-squared            0.2833   Mean dependent var 3314.9
S.E. of regression   1574.1   Akaike info crit.  17.606
Sum squared resid    2E+08    Schwarz criterion  17.706
F-statistic          12.255   Durbin-Watson stat 2.0446
=======================================================
```

a) Consider first model 1. You would like to compare it with a model containing only the dummy variable SEX. Would the two alternative models be nested in each other? Based on the available information and assuming that all other assumptions for OLS are satisfied, could you run a specification test (for $\alpha = 0.05$) allowing you to decide which model to use? Describe the test and the result.

b) When comparing models 1 and 2, are these two models *nested* in each other?

c) What information provided in the output could you use to compare the two models? Based on this information, which model would you choose?

d) Which model specification test, for which the results are reported for both models, could in principle be used to exclude one of the models for further analysis? Does it help in the present application to differentiate between models 1 and 2?

2.3.16. How can the idea of the Hausman test be applied in a situation in which estimators from an OLS regression (with potentially endogenous regressors) as well as estimators from an instrument variable regression (with valid instruments) are available? What is the null hypothesis of this test? When will it be rejected?

2.4 Panel Data

2.4.1. Imagine you would like to collect data on management style for 150 firms in each of the years 2025, 2027 and 2029 by an online survey.

a) What would be the difference between collecting three cross-sectional datasets and one panel dataset?

b) Would it be easier to collect the cross-sectional datasets or the panel dataset? Please justify your answer.

2.4.2. You are given a dataset with $TN = 16232$ observations that is composed of yearly observations t, with $t = 1, \ldots, 4$, for each individual i, with $i = 1, \ldots, 4058$, extracted from the German Socioeconomic Panel (GSOEP) 2009. You conduct a pooled estimation of the following model and obtain the output shown below.

$$\begin{aligned} \texttt{LN\_WAGE\_H}_{i,t} = {} & \beta_0 + \beta_1 \, \texttt{SCHOOLING}_{i,t} + \beta_2 \, \texttt{AGE}_{i,t} + \beta_3 \, \texttt{AGE2}_{i,t} \\ & + \beta_4 \, \texttt{HEALTH}_{i,t} + \beta_5 \, \texttt{DSEX}_{i,t} + \varepsilon_{i,t} \end{aligned}$$

The variables used in the model are defined as follows:

```
LN_WAGE_H i,t: log of hourly wage of i in t
SCHOOLING i,t: years of schooling of i in t
AGE i,t:       age in years of i in t
AGE2 i,t:      squared age of i in t
HEALTH i,t:    health index of i in t
               (smaller values = healthier)
DSEX i,t:      gender dummy of i in t
               (0 = man, 1 = woman)
```

```
==============================================
Dependent Variable: LN_WAGE_H
Method: Panel Least Squares
Sample: 2006 2009
==============================================
Variable      Coeff.  Std.Err.   z-Stat.  Prob.
==============================================
C             0.1017   0.0893    1.1391   0.255
SCHOOLING     0.1083   0.0022    49.376   0.000
AGE           0.0638   0.0040    16.011   0.000
AGE2         -0.0006   4.E-05   -12.834   0.000
HEALTH       -0.0340   0.0045   -7.5626   0.000
DSEX         -0.1930   0.0076   -25.256   0.000
==============================================
R-squared        0.199156  Mean dep. var 2.7561
Adj. R-squar.    0.198909  S.D. dep. var 0.4969
Log likel.     -9876.166   HQ crit.      1.2186
F-statistic      807.0253  Durbin-Watson 0.3479
Prob(F-stat.)    0.000000
==============================================
```

a) Assume for the moment that all assumptions are met. What would be the correct interpretation of the estimated coefficient for SCHOOLING?

b) Is the specific panel data structure considered in a pooled estimation? Which estimation method was used here?

c) Which of the standard assumptions for the linear regression model seems to be violated in such a pooled estimation using this panel dataset? Which test statistic provides an indication of this violation?

2.4.3. Briefly describe the difference of the properties of random and fixed effects estimators (in particular, consistency and efficiency) in dependence of a possible correlation between X and individual specific effects.

How are the individual specific effects in the two models captured?

2.4.4. The following output shows the results of the Wu-Hausman test that compares random and fixed effects estimates for the model presented in Exercise 2.4.2.

```
==================================================================
Correlated Random Effects - Hausman Test
Test cross-section random effects
==================================================================
Test Summary              Chi-Sq. Sta  Chi-Sq. d.f. Prob.
==================================================================
Cross-section random     142.17           4           0.0000
==================================================================
Cross-section random effects test comparisons:
Variable      Fixed       Random      Var(Diff.)    Prob.
==================================================================
SCHOOLING     0.03252     0.10606     0.00029       0.0000
AGE           0.08476     0.06576     0.00003       0.0002
AGE2         -0.00065    -0.00058     0.00000       0.1848
HEALTH       -0.00956    -0.01267     0.00000       0.0023
==================================================================
```

a) State the null hypothesis of the test.

b) Describe how the test statistic is obtained based on the estimators and briefly explain the idea behind the test.

c) Based on the test result, would you recommend estimating a random or fixed effects model? Explain your choice briefly.

2.4.5. Describe two different approaches for estimating a linear regression model with fixed effects when you have panel data covering at least two periods. Will the estimates be numerically identical for a given sample?

2.4.6. You are interested in estimating the gender pay gap in monthly wages after controlling for relevant factors such as working time, education and experience. You have access to a panel data set comprising a large number of individuals over 10 years. To control for unobserved individual heterogeneity, you consider using the fixed effects model. When trying to estimate the (conditional) gender pay gap by the coefficient of the dummy variable for gender, you are likely to receive an error message from the econometric software (e.g., in EViews "Near singular matrix").

a) Explain the reason for this error message.

b) In case of a successful estimation, what is the coefficient for the gender dummy measuring? Is it a sensible estimate of the gender pay gap?

c) Which alternative modeling approach could avoid the issues in a) and b)? Will it always be adequate?

2.4.7. Consider the dynamic panel data model

$$y_{i,t} = \lambda y_{i,t-1} + \boldsymbol{x}'_{i,t}\beta + \alpha_i + u_{i,t} ,$$

where $\eta_{i,t} = \alpha_i + u_{i,t}$ is assumed to be uncorrelated with $x_{i,t}$.

a) Demonstrate that $\eta_{i,t}$ will always be correlated with $y_{i,t-1}$.

b) Provide an approximate estimator of the covariance between $\eta_{i,t}$ and $y_{i,t-1}$ for large values of T, i.e., the number of periods in the panel.

c) Sketch a procedure for estimating the relationship, which results in consistent estimates of β.

2.5 Discrete and Limited Dependent Variables

2.5.1. Which distribution for the error terms is assumed for the Probit model and which for the Logit model?

2.5.2. Name two advantages of the Probit model compared to a Linear Probability Model.

2.5.3. The maximum likelihood function for a Probit estimation can be written as:

$$L(\boldsymbol{\beta}) = \prod_{i=1}^{N} \Phi\left(\boldsymbol{x}_i'\frac{\boldsymbol{\beta}}{\sigma}\right)^{y_i} \left[1 - \Phi\left(\boldsymbol{x}_i'\frac{\boldsymbol{\beta}}{\sigma}\right)\right]^{(1-y_i)}$$

a) Why are $\boldsymbol{\beta}$ and σ not independently identified? What is usually done in order to circumvent this problem when estimating the Probit model?

b) Describe intuitively why maximizing the above likelihood function can be considered as a way to obtain the estimator $\hat{\boldsymbol{\beta}}$ that seems most likely to have generated the observed data. Calculate the log-likelihood function l and the first derivative of the log-likelihood function with respect to β, $\frac{\partial l}{\partial \boldsymbol{\beta}}$. Why is it not possible to solve $\frac{\partial l}{\partial \boldsymbol{\beta}} = \mathbf{0}$ analytically for $\boldsymbol{\beta}$?

2.5.4. The following table shows the results of an estimate to explain the employment chances of individuals.

EMPLOYED	Dummy for having a job (1=Yes, 0=No)
AGE	Age of a person in years
SEX	Dummy for gender (1=female, 0=male)
SCHOOL_T	Number of years spent in school
UNIV	Dummy for having an university degree (1=Yes, 0=No)

```
Dependent Variable: EMPLOYED
Method: ML - Binary Probit (Quadratic hill climbing)
Included observations: 1204
Convergence achieved after 4 iterations
========================================================
Variable   Coefficient   Std. Error  z-Statistic   Prob.
========================================================
C              3.5781       0.5684        6.2950     0.0000
AGE           -0.0543       0.0024       -22.625     0.0000
SEX           -0.4612       0.0391       -11.795     0.0000
SCHOOL_T       0.7177       0.0091        78.868     0.0000
UNIV           0.3149       0.0494        6.3745     0.0000
========================================================
McFadden R-squared     0.4691  Mean dep. var      0.8764
S.D. dependent var     0.4286  S.E. of regres.    0.2741
Akaike info criterion 0.9232  Sum squared res.   1967.7
Schwarz criterion      0.9315  Log likelihood    -3173.3
Hannan-Quinn criter.   0.9311  Restr. log likel.-5977.1
LR statistic           5607.5  Prob(LR stat.)     0.0000
========================================================
```

a) Write down the **complete** underlying model using the usual notation: Y_i for the dependent variable, $X_{1,i}$, $X_{2,i}$, ... for the explanatory variables, and $\beta_1, \beta_2, \ldots$ for the parameters.

b) Is it possible to decide whether having a university degree increases or decreases the probability of having a job significantly ($\alpha = 0.05$)? Explain your answer shortly.

c) Explain briefly what marginal effects are and explain exactly how they can be computed for the variable `SCHOOL_T`. It is not required to provide numerical values.

d) How is the value of the `LR statistic` obtained from other information provided in the output? For what purpose is the `LR statistic` test used? State the null hypothesis of the test. What would your conclusion be based on the outcome of the test?

e) How can the `McFadden R-squared` be computed using information from the output above.

2.5.5. You want to find out what affects firm survival in a year ($y_i = 1$ vs. $y_i = 0$). You have cross sectional data for 1.254 firms and the year 2023 and decide to apply the probit model (note that we assume $\sigma_u^2 = 1$ for identification):

$$y_i = \begin{cases} 1 & \text{if } \; y_i^* = x_i'\beta + u_i > 0 \\ 0 & \text{otherwise} \end{cases}, \text{ where } u \overset{iid}{\sim} \mathcal{N}(0, \sigma_u^2 = 1)$$

a) One variable included in the vector x is the debt ratio of the firm (i.e. total debt divided by total assets). Please suggest two further variables that you expect to have a significant impact on the probability of a company surviving the business year. Provide a brief economic explanation of your choice and the expected sign of the effect.

b) What could be an economic interpretation of the latent variable y_i^* in the model?

c) Show that $E(y_i) = \Phi(x_i'\beta)$, where $\Phi(\cdot)$ denotes the cumulative distribution function of a standard normal distribution.

d) After being provided with all necessary data for the 1254 firms, you have run a probit estimation and obtained the results shown in Table 2.1.

```
Dependent Variable: Y
Method: ML - Binary Probit (Quadratic hill climbing)
Included observations: 1254
Convergence achieved after 5 iterations
Covariance matrix computed using second derivatives
=====================================================
            Coefficient  Std.Error  z-Statistic  Prob.
=====================================================
C(1)          2.947396   0.268343   10.98369    0.0000
C(2)          1.979898   0.169821   11.65873    0.0000
C(3)         -0.984506   0.085508  -11.51367    0.0000
C(4)          0.555611   0.054124   10.26561    0.0000
=====================================================
McFadden R-squared    0.7547  Mean dependent var 0.7850
S.D. dependent var    0.4110  S.E. of regression 0.2004
Akaike info crit.     0.2634  Sum squared resid  39.998
Schwarz criterion     0.2830  Log likelihood    -127.70
Hannan-Quinn criter.  0.2709  Deviance           255.40
Restr. deviance       1041.0  Restr.log likelih -520.51
LR statistic          785.61  Avg.log likelihoo -0.1277
Prob(LR statistic)    0.0000
=====================================================
```

Table 2.1. Estimation results from binary probit model.

Assume that the third coefficient C(3) in the output corresponds to a variable measuring the debt ratio of the firm (i.e. total debt divided by total assets).

- Is it possible to conclude from the value of the coefficient whether the debt ratio has a positive or negative effect on the probability of surviving the business year? If yes, what is the direction of influence?

- Explain briefly whether you can make a decision on the null hypothesis that the actual effect of the debt ratio is zero (i.e. H_0: C(3) = 0) at level $\alpha = 0.05$; if yes, how would you decide?
- The software also provides you with the value −0.23 for the following expression:

$$\frac{1}{N}\sum_{i=1}^{N}\phi(x_i'\beta)\beta_3\,,$$

where β_3 refers to `C(3)` and $\phi(\cdot)$ denotes the density function of a standard normal distribution. How can this value be interpreted (you may start your explanation with looking at a single summand of the sum).

e) Table 2.2 shows an expectation-prediction evaluation for the estimated model from d).

```
==============================================================
Expectation-Prediction Evaluation for Binary Specification
Success cutoff: C = 0.5
==============================================================
               Estimated Equation        Constant Probability
               Dep=0   Dep=1   Total   Dep=0   Dep=1   Total
==============================================================
P(Dep=1)<=C       44      36      80       0       0       0
P(Dep=1)>C       171     749     920     215     785    1000
Total            215     785    1000     215     785    1000
Correct           44     749     793       0     785     785
% Correct      20.47   95.41   79.30    0.00  100.00   78.50
% Incorrect    79.53    4.59   20.70  100.00    0.00   21.50
Total Gain*    20.47   -4.59    0.80
Percent Gain** 20.47      NA    3.72
==============================================================
```

Table 2.2. Expectation-prediction evaluation for probit model.

- How many firms survived the business year 2023 ($y_i = 1$)?
- What is the meaning of the `Success cutoff` value `C=0.5`?
- Which provides better predictions: the probit model or a naive model that assumes all companies survive the business year? Please briefly explain your answer.

2.5.6. Assume that you estimate an ordered Probit model with three possible outcomes of the dependent variable y_i. You obtain estimates of the parameter vector $\hat{\beta}$ for the latent model and the thresholds shown in the equation below based on the assumption that the variance of the error terms in the latent model is one:

$$y_i = \begin{cases} 0, & \text{if } y_i^* \leq 0 \\ 1, & \text{if } 0 < y_i^* \leq 0.5 \\ 2, & \text{if } y_i^* > 0.5 \end{cases}$$

Furthermore, assume that for an individual i the values of the explanatory variables in $\boldsymbol{x}_i$ are known but not the value of y_i. Finally, assume that for observation i $\boldsymbol{x}_i'\hat{\boldsymbol{\beta}} = 1$.

a) What are the predicted probabilities for $y_i = 0$, $y_i = 1$ and $y_i = 2$ for this observation?

b) Mark the appropriate areas in the standard normal distribution shown in Figure 2.2. (Hint: the standard normal distribution below refers to the distribution of the error term ε_j.)

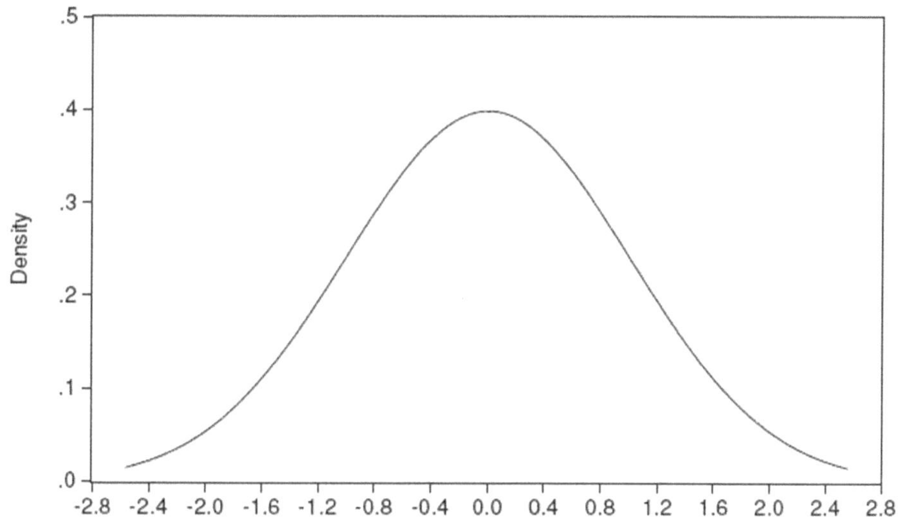

Fig. 2.2. Density function of stanard normally distributed error terms.

c) Assume that the estimate of parameter β_k for the explanatory variable x_k in $\boldsymbol{x}$ is positive. What general conclusion can you draw on the effect of a one unit increase of x_k on the probabilities of y to be 0, 1, or 2?

2.5.7. Jüttler *et al.* (2025) analyze the impact of economic competencies on study program choices. To this end, they collected data for Swiss students at two different time periods. First, shortly before graduating from school, indicators of economic competencies were measured. Second, five years later, students were asked about further study programs. These were categorized into "(1) humanities and social sciences (HS), (2) economics (EC), (3) law, (4) medicine (Med), (5) exact, natural, and technical sciences (ENT) and (6) other" (OT).

Table 2.3 shows an excerpt of Table 6 in Jüttler *et al.* (2025, p. 199) based on 1,077 observations. The coefficients are provided as odds ratios. Bold face indicates statistically significant differences to 1 at least at the 10% level.

	Model 1				
	HS	Law	Med	ENT	OT
Economic knowledge and skills	**0.54**	**0.55**	**0.45**	0.83	**0.63**
Interest in economics	0.80	**0.46**	0.76	0.56	**0.56**
Intrinsic motivation regarding economics	1.24	**2.61**	1.15	2.07	**1.94**
Attitude toward economics	0.64	0.78	1.17	0.49	0.61
Value-oriented disposition (in economics)	1.02	1.08	1.00	0.98	0.85

Table 2.3. Excerpt from Table 6 in Jüttler *et al.* (2025, p.199).

a) Why did the authors use a multinomial logit model instead of an ordered probit model (1 - 6) for the study programs?

b) Below the table in the article, you find the note: "Reference group is economics". Explain the role of the reference group in the multinomial logit model.

c) Interpret the coefficient for *Economic knowledge and skills* for the outcome *Law* (0.55).

d) Are students with higher intrinsic motivation regarding economics ceteris paribus more likely to study economics as compared to other study programs?

2.5.8. Derive formally what happens with the expected value of a censored normal distribution with increasing degree of censoring. How does this finding translate to a regression model with censored y variable?

2.5.9. Name and describe a regression model for censored data. Indicate an application for which using the model is preferable in comparison to a standard linear regression model. Briefly justify your answer.

2.5.10. Table 2.4 shows the estimation results for two models based on simulated data. Thereby 1 000 observations were generated according to the following data generating process (DGP):

$$x_i \sim N(0;1) \text{ and } \varepsilon_i \sim N(0;0.25)$$
$$y_i^* = -0.5 + 0.5x + \epsilon_i$$
$$y_i = \begin{cases} 0, & \text{if } y_i^* \leq 0 \\ y_i^*, & \text{if } y_i^* > 0 \end{cases}$$

Model 1:

```
Dependent Variable: Y                            Method: Least Squares
Sample: 1 1000
Included observations: 1000
============================================================
    Variable       CoefficientStd. Errort-Statistic  Prob.
============================================================
        C            0.105096   0.006899   15.23453   0.0000
        X            0.116718   0.006719   17.37108   0.0000
============================================================
```

Model 2:

```
Dependent Variable: Y                            Method: Least Squares
Sample: 1 1000 IF Y>0
Included observations: 244
============================================================
    Variable       CoefficientStd. Errort-Statistic  Prob.
============================================================
        C            0.284044   0.029980   9.474374   0.0000
        X            0.154709   0.024097   6.420394   0.0000
============================================================
```

Table 2.4. Estimation results for simulated data.

Discuss why the two outputs deliver an argument in favor of the usage of the Tobit model.

2.5.11 Briefly explain the selection effect that can occur when we want to estimate a treatment effect. What could be the consequence if this selection effect is ignored?

2.5.12. Table 2.5 provides the results of an estimate aiming at explaining the net wages of employed women (NET_WAGE). Thereby, the explanatory variables are:

FORMATION: Years of schooling plus years of vocational training
JOB_EXPER: Job experience in years
DEAST: Dummy for Eastern Germany (= 1 for Eastern Germany)
NATIOND: Dummy to capture German nationality (= 1 for Germans)

a) Describe the meaning of the variable MILLS_RATIO in the output, i.e., the procedure to generate this variable.

```
Dependent Variable: NET_WAGE     Method: Least Squares
Included observations: 5301
======================================================
Variable     Coefficient Std. Error  z-Statistic  Prob.
------------------------------------------------------
C              650.5742    127.1956     5.114754  0.0000
FORMATION      77.09668    5.613550     13.73403  0.0000
JOB_EXPER      2.876223    1.270718     2.263463  0.0236
DEAST         -10.39639    21.62607    -0.480734  0.6307
DGERMAN        313.0605    42.38750     7.385680  0.0000
MILLS_RATIO -1273.407     99.72362    -12.76937  0.0000
======================================================
R-squared            0.2200  Mean dependent var  1125.53
Adjusted R-squared 0.2192  S.D. dependent var  740.785
======================================================
```

Table 2.5. Estimation results for net wages of employed women.

b) Explain under which circumstances this variable should be included in the model and possible consequences if it is omitted.

Part II

Sample Solutions for Selected Exercises

3

Solutions for Multiple Choice Questions

In this chapter, you will find all sample solutions to the single-choice, true or false, and completion questions. Some solutions are accompanied by brief additional explanations. The sample solutions are intended to help you assess your own performance. You should try to solve the exercises independently or with the help of a textbook before consulting the sample solutions. The numbering of the solutions corresponds to the numbering of the questions.

3.0 Matrix Algebra and Principles of Inferential Statistics

Matrix Algebra

1.0.1. d)

1.0.2. idempotent, symmetric

1.0.3. a)

1.0.4. b)

1.0.5. a) True; to verify this, you can calculate AA and see that it is equal to A.

1.0.6. d) The dimensions of A (2×2) and B' (4×2) do not allow their multiplication. Thus, the matrix $AB'BC$ is not defined, i.e., it is not a 2×4 matrix.

Principles of Inferential Statistics

1.0.7. b)

1.0.8. a)

1.0.9. c)

1.0.10. Central Limit Theorem; Fundamental Theorem of Statistics

P. Winker, *Exercise Book Advanced Econometrics*,
https://doi.org/10.1007/978-3-662-74252-5_3

3.1 Aspects of (Micro)econometric Analyses

The Role of Econometrics

1.1.1. b)

1.1.2. a)

1.1.3. d)

1.1.4. a) Regarding option d), it should be noted that σ^2 is also unknown and has to be estimated from the sample. Thus, the t-statistic does not follow the standard normal distribution, but the t-distribution with $N-1$ degrees of freedom. Only for N going to infinity, this distribution is equivalent to the standard normal distribution.

What is Special about Microeconomic Data?

1.1.5. c)

1.1.6. b) False

1.1.7. a) Please note that the question is formulated in a negative way (that is, why the word "not" is printed in bold). Thus, we are looking for the wrong statement. The sampling issues (b)), nonlinear relationships (c)) and non-normal distribution (d)) are common issues of data at the microlevel. However, microlevel data typically fit better to theoretical concepts compared to aggregates (e.g., the price of a liter of water is a precise measure in a microeconomic model of water demand, while the GDP-deflator is a complex construct used to reflect the price level p in macroeconomic models; therefore, a) is the correct answer as it suggests that the data do **not** fit well with the theoretical concepts.

1.1.8. a) True

1.1.9. d)

3.2 Estimation

Ordinary Least Squares

1.2.1. a)

1.2.2. b)

1.2.3. d)

1.2.4. c)

1.2.5. a)

1.2.6. d)

1.2.7. a) True

1.2.8. d) R^2 measures how much of the variation in Y is explained by the model. If the variance of Y is about the same as the variance of the error terms U, almost nothing of the variation of Y is explained. Thus, R^2 will be close to zero.

1.2.9. a) Given the almost perfectly linear relationship, A should correspond to the largest value, while C still exhibits a strong, but weaker linear relationship. Thus, $A > C$. B seems to exhibit structure, but is nonlinear, while D shows only a minor negative slope. Consequently, $A > C > D > B$ is the answer that best corresponds to the datasets presented.

1.2.10. a)

Nonlinear Least Squares

1.2.11. b)

1.2.12. b) The relationship shown in a) is already linear in the parameters: Just think of two explanatory variables $x_{1,i} = x_i$ and $x_{2,i} = x_i^3$. Then, the model would read $y_i = \beta_0 + \beta_1 x_{2,i} + \beta_2 x_{2,i} + u_i$, which is a linear model and can be estimated by OLS. For c), taking the natural logarithm on both sides of the equation results in $\ln y_i = \ln \alpha_0 + \alpha_1 \ln x_{1,i} + \alpha_2 \ln x_{2,i} + \ln u_i$, which is also a linear model and can be estimated by OLS. Finally, for d), the model can be rewritten as

$$y_i^2 = \alpha_1 + 2\alpha_1\alpha_2 x_i + \alpha_2^2 x_i^2 + 2\alpha_1 u_i + 2\alpha_2 x_i u_i + u_i^2 = (\alpha_1 + \alpha_2 x_i + u_i)^2 .$$

Consequently, taking the square root on both sides of the equation results in a standard linear regression model $y_i = \alpha_1 + \alpha_2 x_i + u_i$, which can be estimated by OLS.

1.2.13. b) is the answer as the statement provided is not correct: According to the output shown, the estimated model was $C_t^2 = \alpha_1^2 + 2\alpha_1\alpha_2 Y_i^d + \alpha_2^2 \left(Y_i^d\right)^2 + u_t^2$. In contrast, d) is a correct answer, since instead of estimating the model for C_t^2, you could take the square root on both sides and estimate $C_t = \alpha_1 + \alpha_2 Y_i^d$ by ordinary least squares.

Generalized Least Squares

1.2.14. b) Since $\text{Var}(\Omega^{-1/2}u) = E(\Omega^{-1/2}u(\Omega^{-1/2}u)') = \Omega^{-1/2}\Omega(\Omega^{-1/2})' = \Omega^{-1/2}(\Omega^{-1})^{-1}(\Omega^{-1/2})' = \Omega^{-1/2}((\Omega^{-1/2})'\Omega^{-1/2})^{-1}(\Omega^{-1/2})' = \Omega^{-1/2}\Omega^{1/2}(\Omega^{1/2})'(\Omega^{-1/2})' = I = constant$

1.2.15. d)

1.2.16. d) Note that variables in X that are not correlated with u can be instrumented "by themselves".

1.2.17. b)

1.2.18. b) Although a low value of R^2 might be an indication of a week instrument, it does not preclude the second step of the IV estimation. Therefore, the statement is not correct and, consequently, is the answer to the question.

Maximum Likelihood

1.2.19. a)

1.2.20. d) This statement is not correct for ML in the general case, but only for the linear model with normally distributed error term.

1.2.21. c)

1.2.22. a)

1.2.23. a)

General Method of Moments

1.2.24. b) Note that a) is not correct since for GMM the objective function has to be minimized and not to be maximized.

1.2.25. d) $\Omega^{-1/2}Y = \Omega^{-1/2}X\beta + \Omega^{-1/2}u = Y^* = X^*\beta + u^*$
$\Rightarrow \hat{\beta}_{GLS} = (X^{*\prime}X^*)^{-1}X^{*\prime}Y^* = (X'\Omega^{-1}X)^{-1}X'\Omega^{-1}$

1.2.26. d)

3.3 Hypothesis Testing and Model Selection

Linear Hypothesis

1.3.1. c); Note that b) can be rewritten as $\beta_1 = 3\beta_2$,i.e., as a linear hypothesis.

1.3.2. d)

1.3.3. a); b) is not correct as the estimates of the variance differ even if a normal distribution of error terms is assumed.

1.3.4. a); d) might be a tempting option for people aware of the different scales of both variables (Worktime per week, wage income per month). However, the interpretation given in d) is correct since it is the usual marginal effect, i.e., increasing the explanatory variable by 1 unit on its scale goes in line with an increase of the dependent variable by the size of the parameter in its scale. Thus, d) is correct.

1.3.5. d); To check whether the coefficient of a single variable is significantly different from zero, one can resort directly to the t-statistic or empirical p-value (`Prob`) provided in the estimation output. Thus, we can conclude that the effect of `@SEAS(1)` is statistically significant different from zero. The effect is negative. Hence, statement a) is correct. We can also infer that the null hypothesis `R3M`= 0 cannot be rejected at the 5% level. Thus, also statement c) is correct. For solution b), we have to calculate the relevant t-statistic ourselves. It amounts to $\frac{0.901954-1}{0.015574} = -6.9255$. Comparing this value in absolute terms with the t-distribution with $60-7=53$ degrees of freedom or the good approximation by a standard normal distribution will result in a rejection. Thus, statement b) is also correct. Given that d) is a statement about the joint significance of two variables, running an appropriate F-test for the two parameters would be required. The results of such a test are not provided. Thus, we cannot confirm that the last statement is correct. Please note that the F-statistic provided in the output corresponds to the null hypothesis that all coefficients except for the constant are equal to zero, which could be rejected.

1.3.6. b)

1.3.7. c)

General Hypothesis

1.3.8. b)

1.3.9. a)

1.3.10. c)

1.3.11. b) The distance marked **B** is related to the Wald statistic. However, the WAld statistic is constructed as the weighted sum of squared deviations from the restriction. In a univariate setting as shown in the figure, it would be proportional to $\mathbf{B}^2$ and not to **B**.

1.3.12. d)

Hypothesis about Model Assumptions

1.3.13. a); The Jarque-Bera statistic is used to testing the assumption that the error terms follow a normal distribution.

1.3.14. c); Both the test statistic of the LR test and the Wald test are large compared to a χ^2-distribution with 5 degrees of freedom, which is reflected in the very small p-values. Therefore, the null hypothesis of no structural break has to be rejected. Thus, statement c) is not correct.

1.3.15. c)

1.3.16. b)

1.3.17. a); The Durbin-Watson is for no autocorrelation of error terms; The Lilliefor's test could only be applied to residuals $\hat{u}$, and the reference distribution would not be standard normal, but a normal distribution with the variance of the residuals.

1.3.18. b)

1.3.19. Ramsey RESET-test; powers (or: a polynomial)

1.3.20. b); c) is correct since the indicated degrees of freedom (df) correspond to $N - K$ and $K = 5$.

1.3.21. b) Running the model with cross terms would add linear terms (except for the dummies) and cross-products of variables to the test equation. Then, the number of degrees of freedom would be much larger than 4. For the test equation without cross terms, only the four squared explanatory variables are included, which corresponds to four degrees of freedom as indicated in the test output.

1.3.22. White-test of heteroskedasticity; homoskedastic; has to be

1.3.23. a)

1.3.24. b); a) The empirical cumulative distribution function at zero has a value of approximately 0.35, i.e., substantially less than 50% of all residuals are negative.

1.3.25. b); a) if all tests are independent, you will end up with an expected number of rejections of about 18.55% and an absolute maximum of 20%; if they are correlated, it will be less; c) if they are independent, this happens in $0.05^4 = 0.000625\%$ of all repetitions; if they are correlated it could be more, but never more than 5%, which happens with perfect correlation (d)).

Model Selection

1.3.26. d)

1.3.27. b) Information criteria such as AIC or BIC are used to compare different models. When applied to the same model, they just differ due to the different penalty terms, which does not allow for any conclusion regarding model fit.

1.3.28. nested; t-test; including

1.3.29. d); a comparison of R^2 makes sense, given that both models have the same number of parameters. Therefore, the negative statement in c) is wrong.

3.4 Panel Data

1.4.1. a) True; constructing a panel requires following the firms over time, which is more challenging than collecting three cross-sectional datasets.

1.4.2. d); a) pooled estimators ignore individual specific effects, b) fixed effects estimation is always possible in a balanced panel, c) this is the number of individuals in each wave of the panel.

1.4.3. b) False; it is feasible, but it might not be the best option.

1.4.4. autocorrelation; Durbin-Watson

1.4.5. a)

1.4.6. b)

1.4.7. d)

3.5 Discrete and Limited Dependent Variables

1.5.1. a)

1.5.2. c)

1.5.3. d)

1.5.4. d)

1.5.5. a)

1.5.6. c)

4 Solutions for Open Exercises

In this chapter, you will find sample solutions or solution hints to some of the open questions in Chapter 2. The sample solutions are intended to help you assess your own performance. You should try to solve the exercises independently or with the help of a textbook before consulting the sample solutions. The numbering of the solutions corresponds to the numbering of the questions.

4.0 Matrix Algebra and Principles of Inferential Statistics

Matrix Algebra

2.0.1. The admissible dimensions are as follows:

a) all $N \in \mathbb{N}^+$

b) $N = K$

c) any $N, K \in \mathbb{N}^+$

d) any $N, K \in \mathbb{N}^+$

e) any $N = K$

2.0.2. $rank(A) = 3$, $trace(A) = 16$, $rank(B) = 3$, $trace(B)$ not defined, $rank(C) = 2$, $trace(C) = 4$

2.0.3. Start with the definition of M and then simplify:

P. Winker, *Exercise Book Advanced Econometrics*,
https://doi.org/10.1007/978-3-662-74252-5_4

$$
\begin{aligned}
MM &= (I - X(X'X)^{-1}X')(I - X(X'X)^{-1}X') \\
&= I - 2X(X'X)^{-1}X' + X(X'X)^{-1}\underbrace{X'X(X'X)^{-1}}_{=I}X' \\
&= I - 2X(X'X)^{-1}X' + X(X'X)^{-1}X' \\
&= I - X(X'X)^{-1}X' = M
\end{aligned}
$$

Principles of Inferential Statistics

2.0.4. The central idea of the law of large numbers is that as the sample size increases, the sample mean converges to the true population mean, i.e., if $\bar{X}_n$ denotes the mean of a sample of size n, $\bar{X}_n \xrightarrow{p} \mu \quad \text{as } n \to \infty$.

2.0.5. The central theorem of statistics claims that for random drawings from a distribution, the empirical distribution function converges to the theoretical (true) distribution function as the number of drawings goes to infinity. The idea of a proof is to consider any quantile X_p of the true distribution function and the indicator variable $I(X < X_p)$ that takes the value 1 if a random drawing X is smaller than X_p. According to the law of large numbers, the mean of these indicator values, which corresponds to the frequency of $X < X_p$ converges to the expected value, which is equal to p. As this holds for any p between 0 and 1, the empirical distribution converges to the true one.

2.0.6. a) Normal as sum of normally distributed random numbers

b) Triangular shape

c) The sum of many independently distributed random numbers converges to a normal distribution according to the central limit theorem.

d) The sum of four squared standard normally distributed random numbers is χ^2 distributed with 4 degrees of freedom.

2.0.7. a) Denote the limits of the interval by lb and ub, respectively. Then, the following condition should hold:

$$
\begin{aligned}
Prob(lb \leq \quad \mu \quad \leq ub) &= 0.95 \\
Prob(-lb \geq \quad -\mu \quad \geq -ub) &= 0.95 \\
\Leftrightarrow Prob(\bar{x} - lb \geq \bar{x} - \mu \geq \bar{x} - ub) &= 0.95 \\
\Leftrightarrow Prob\left(\frac{\bar{x} - lb}{\hat{\sigma}} \geq \underbrace{\frac{\bar{x} - \mu}{\hat{\sigma}}}_{\sim t_{n-1}} \geq \frac{\bar{x} - ub}{\hat{\sigma}}\right) &= 0.95
\end{aligned}
$$

It follows that $\frac{\bar{x}-lb}{\hat{\sigma}} = t_{n-1};0.975$ and $\frac{\bar{x}-lb}{\hat{\sigma}} = t_{n-1};0.025 = -t_{n-1};0.975$ and, consequently, that $lb = \bar{x}-t_{n-1};0.975*\hat{\sigma}$ and $ub = \bar{x}+t_{n-1};0.975*\hat{\sigma}$, where $t_{n-1};0.975*\hat{\sigma}$ denotes the 97.5% quantile of the t-distribution with $n-1$ degrees of freedom. For large n this is well approximated by the 97.5% quantile of the standard normal distribution. In this case, i.e., for large n (≥ 30), the confidence interval becomes $[\bar{x} - 1.96\hat{\sigma}; \bar{x} + 1.96\hat{\sigma}]$

b) Becomes larger; shifts to the right; becomes smaller.

c) No sample solution.

d) No sample solution.

4.1 Approach and Principles of Econometric Modeling

The Role of Econometrics

2.1.1. No sample solution.

2.1.2. No sample solution.

2.1.3. No sample solution.

2.1.4. The central ingredients of any econometric analysis are economic theory, data, and statistical methods. Economic theory is essential for setting up the model and provides arguments for causal reasoning versus focus just on (conditional) correlations. The availability and quality of the data will also have a major effect on the outcome. Finally, depending on the model and the available data, appropriate statistical methods have to be selected.

2.1.5. No sample solution.

2.1.6. a) The structural parameters are $\beta_0, \beta_1, \beta_2, \sigma_{\varepsilon_C}, \gamma_0, \gamma_1, \sigma_{\varepsilon_I}$. It is also important to include the variances

b) The reduced form can be obtained by solving the system of equations with regard to the three endogenous variables $C_t, I_t, andY_t$. We obtain

$$\begin{aligned} C_t &= \alpha_{C1} + \alpha_{C2}G_t + \alpha_{C3}r_t + \nu_{C,t} \\ I_t &= \alpha_{I1} + \alpha_{I2}G_t + \alpha_{I3}r_t + \nu_{I,t} \\ Y_t &= \alpha_{Y1} + \alpha_{Y2}G_t + \alpha_{Y3}r_t + \nu_{Y,t} \end{aligned}$$

where, e.g., $\alpha_{C1} = \frac{\beta_0+\beta_1\gamma_0}{1-\beta_1}$, $\alpha_{C2} = \frac{\beta_1}{1-\beta_1}$, and $\alpha_{C3} = \frac{\beta_1\gamma_1+\beta_2}{1-\beta_1}$.

c) All α_{XY} and the variances of all ν_X

d) Yes, at least for some of them, e.g., from α_{C2} you can obtain $\beta_1 = \frac{\alpha_{C2}}{1-\alpha_{C2}}$.

What is Special about Microeconomic Data?

2.1.7. No sample solution. Hint: A key aspect is the difference between randomly selected subsets and the condition resulting in the specific subset shown in panel B.

2.1.8. No sample solution.

2.1.9. No sample solution.

4.2 Estimation

Ordinary Least Squares

2.2.1. The result can be derived using the definition of the OLS estimator:

$$\begin{aligned}\hat{\beta} &= (X'X)^{-1}X'Y \\ &= (X'X)^{-1}X'(X\beta + u) \\ &= (X'X)^{-1}(X'X)\beta + (X'X)^{-1}X'u \\ &= \beta + (X'X)^{-1}X'u \\ \Rightarrow E(\hat{\beta}|X) &= \beta + E((X'X)^{-1}X'u|X) = \beta \\ &\text{due to } E(X'u) = 0\end{aligned}$$

2.2.2. The notation includes the requirements of normal distribution, homoskedasticity, and no autocorrelation. For example, if the condition of "no autocorrelation" is not satisfied, t- or F-statistics under H_0 will not follow the relevant t- or F-distribution.

Nonlinear Least Squares

2.2.3. a) If you apply the natural logarithm on both sides of the equation, you obtain a linear regression model for the logarithm of the real output. The parameters of central interest, α and β, remain unchanged and can be estimated by OLS.

b) Using the linearized version avoids potential numerical problems of NLS.

2.2.4. a) $Y_t = e^{\beta_1} K_t^{\beta_2} L_t^{\beta_3} + u_t$.

b) The coefficients correspond to the production elasticities of capital (β_2) and labor (β_3), respectively. If all assumptions of the nonlinear regression model are satisfied, statements on statistical significance (i.e., the null hypothesis H_0: $\beta_i = 0$) can be made based on the t-statistic. The null hypothesis can be rejected for both parameters at the 5% level, i.e., they are statistically significant different from zero.

2.2.5. a) No sample solution. Hint: Tests for statistical significance require that all assumptions about the model and the estimator are satisfied.

b) No sample solution. Hint: A relevant benchmark is the "no returns to scale" situation, when both parameters add up to one.

c) No sample solution. Hint: Keep in mind that using numerical methods for obtaining estimates does not always guaranty to deliver the theoretically defined estimator.

Generalized Least Squares

2.2.6. a) No, because the error terms are heteroscedastic, since $\Omega = E(uu') \neq \sigma^2 I$. For the variance of $\hat{\beta}$ one obtains:

$$
\begin{aligned}
Var(\hat{\beta}) &= E[(\hat{\beta} - \beta)(\hat{\beta} - \beta)'] \\
&= E[((X'X)^{-1}X'(X\beta + u) - \beta)((X'X)^{-1}X'(X\beta + u) - \beta)'] \\
&= E[((X'X)^{-1}X'X\beta + (X'X)^{-1}X'u - \beta)\cdot \\
&\qquad ((X'X)^{-1}X'X\beta + (X'X)^{-1}X'u - \beta)'] \\
&= E[\beta + (X'X)^{-1}X'u - \beta)(\beta + (X'X)^{-1}X'u - \beta)'] \\
&= E[(X'X)^{-1}X'uu'X(X'X)^{-1}] \\
&= (X'X)^{-1}X'E[uu']X(X'X)^{-1} \\
&= (X'X)^{-1}X'\Omega X(X'X)^{-1}
\end{aligned}
$$

b) The covariance matrix of the error terms u is given by Ω, containing the variances of the individual error terms on the main diagonal, while all other entries (covariances) are assumed to be equal to zero:

$$
\Omega = \begin{bmatrix} \sigma_1^2 & 0 & \cdots & 0 \\ 0 & \sigma_2^2 & \cdots & 0 \\ \vdots & \vdots & \ddots & \vdots \\ 0 & 0 & \cdots & \sigma_n^2 \end{bmatrix} \Rightarrow \Omega^{-1} = \begin{bmatrix} \frac{1}{\sigma_1^2} & 0 & \cdots & 0 \\ 0 & \frac{1}{\sigma_2^2} & \cdots & 0 \\ \vdots & \vdots & \ddots & \vdots \\ 0 & 0 & \cdots & \frac{1}{\sigma_n^2} \end{bmatrix}
$$

The Cholesky factor P ofΩ^{-1} is also a diagonal matrix, i.e., $P = P'$ given by

$$P = \begin{bmatrix} \frac{1}{\sigma_1} & 0 & \cdots & 0 \\ 0 & \frac{1}{\sigma_2} & \cdots & 0 \\ \vdots & \vdots & \ddots & \vdots \\ 0 & 0 & & \frac{1}{\sigma_n} \end{bmatrix}$$

By premultiplying the model with P, we divide each observation by the standard error of the corresponding error term u_i. Consequently, the higher the error variance, the bigger the denominator, which implies that compared to OLS, we give less weight to the observations that have a high variance and more weight to the observations that have a small variance.

c) No sample solution. Hint: Note that the new error terms $u^* = Pu$ are homoscedastic.

d) This is an application of the general setting described in a). The variances are assumed to increase with the values of x_i, i.e., from left to right. Consequently, a GLS estimator would place less emphasis on the observations further to the right, which might result in a slightly flatter regression line.

e) No sample solution.

2.2.7. a) The central idea is to overcome the indirect effect of the error terms u on y through the correlation with the variables in $\boldsymbol{X}$. To this end, $\boldsymbol{X}$ is replaced by a forecast of $\boldsymbol{X}$ based on variables that are not correlated with u, the so-called *instruments*. In addition to not being correlated with u, instruments should be correlated with $\boldsymbol{X}$ to provide good forecasts of $\boldsymbol{X}$.

b) There are several methods available, including two-stage least squares (TSLS) and FGLS. The model can also be estimated by GMM.

2.2.8. a) Hint: No complex calculations are required. Focus on the information provided in the output.

b) The method mentioned in the output is `Two-Stage Least Squares`, i.e., a model with instrumental variables is estimated. A reason for this choice would be the assumption of a correlation between error terms and the explanatory variable "time spent in schooling". For example, unobserved characteristics of the individuals, such as motivation to work or fun with learning, might affect both time spent in schooling and actual wage income.

c) The output does not present evidence for the necessity of using instruments, nor does it present evidence whether the chosen instruments are good ones.

d) No sample solution.

Maximum Likelihood

2.2.9. For OLS, the objective is to **minimize** the sum of squared differences between observations and model forecasts. For ML, the objective is to **maximize** the likelihood function that reflects the likelihood (in case of discrete dependent variables, actually the probability) of observing what is observed.

2.2.10. a) No sample solution.

b) No sample solution.

c) No sample solution.

Generalized Method of Moments

2.2.11. No sample solution.

2.2.12. a) No sample solution.

b) No sample solution.

c) No sample solution.

2.2.13. The GMM estimator does not require a specific assumption about the distribution of the error terms $\boldsymbol{u}$. Furthermore, the quadratic objective function to be minimized might be less challenging for numerical procedures than more complex likelihood functions in the ML approach.

4.3 Hypothesis Testing and Model Selection

Linear Hypothesis

2.3.1. a) t-test for H_0^1 and H_0^2, and F-test for H_0^4. Note that the condition in H_0^2 could be rewritten as $\beta_1 - 2\beta_2 = 0$, i.e., a linear constraint.

b) For example, for H_0^2: $\boldsymbol{R} = [01 - 2...0]$ and $r = 0$.

2.3.2. In the OLS framework, the t-statistic follows exactly the t-distribution with the corresponding number of degrees of freedom. For the ML setting, only the asymptotic distribution for the sample size going to infinity is known to be normal.

General Hypothesis

2.3.3. a) No sample solution

b) The tests require different inputs. For the Wald-test, only the unrestricted model has to be estimated, while for the LM-test only the restricted model has to be estimated. In settings, where one of the two models is easy to estimate, while the other one is more challenging, a suitable choice of the test can reduce numerical issues. For example, a test focusing on non-linear components of the model to be present or not, might be a candidate for the LM-approach as estimated the restricted, in this case linear, model might be easier.

2.3.4. a) When all assumptions for the linear regression model are satisfied including the assumption of a normal distribution of the error terms.

b) In this case, the exact distribution of the F-statistic would be known (the F-distribution), while for the Wald-test only asymptotic inference would be available.

2.3.5. a) For the LR-test: Mark the unrestricted ML estimator ($\hat{\theta}_U$) on the θ-axis corresponding to the maximum of the log-likelihood function. Mark the restricted estimator ($\tilde{\theta}_R$) corresponding to the value for which $c(\theta) = 0$. For both estimates, mark the corresponding values of the log-likelihood and highlight the difference between both values which is proportional to the LR statistic.

For the Wald-test: Use the unrestricted estimator $\hat{\theta}_U$ and mark the value of the constraint function c for this value, i.e., $c(\hat{\theta}_U)$, which should be small under the null hypothesis. Note that the Wald statistic will be calculated as a weighted average of the squares of these values of constraint violations.

b) When calculating the constrained estimator is difficult.

2.3.6. a) The assumption of homoscedastic error terms. The null hypothesis is that error terms are homoscedastic, i.e., have the same variance for all observations. The test used is the **White-**test. The idea of the test is to consider an alternative making the variance of error terms depending on explanatory variables, squares of explanatory variables and cross-term (version with cross terms) or just the squares of the explanatory variables (version without cross terms). If all these potential factors jointly do not help to "explain" the error variance approximated by the squared residuals u_i^2, the null hypothesis does not has to be rejected.

b) The test statistic in the second row of the test output is the R^2 of the test equation multiplied with the number of observations and should be small compared to a χ^2-distribution with the number of degrees of freedom equal to the explanatory variables in the test equation (8 in the application). The test statistic is larger than the 95% quantile of the chi^2-distribution with 8 df (p-value below 0.05). Consequently, the null hypothesis of homoscedastic error terms has to be rejected.

c) Including all variables, squared variables and interaction terms would result in perfect multicollinearity as `DSMOKER` and `DSMOKER^2` have exactly the same values as for any dummy variable. Therefore, only `DSMOKER^2` is included in the test equation

d) $RENT_i = \beta_0 + \beta_1 WAGE\_M_i + \beta_2 NR\_CHILD_i + \beta_3 DSMOKER_i + u_i.$

2.3.7. a) If all assumptions for the specific model are satisfied, the z-statistic provided in the output for the variable `WAGE` allows testing the null hypothesis that the corresponding coefficient in the population is equal to zero. Given the absolute size of the test-statistic (and the corresponding p-value 0.0003), the null hypothesis has to be rejected at the 5% level and a significant impact of `WAGE` is found. The negative sign of the coefficient indicates that higher `WAGE` ceteris paribus reduces the probability of renting an apartment (rather than owning one). Note that in the Probit model shown, the size of the coefficient cannot be interpreted directly as marginal effect on the probability.

b) `Log Likelihood` is the value of the log-likelihood function for the estimated model, `Restr. log likel.` is the value of the log-likelihood function for a model containing solely a constant. The `LR Statistic` is equal to two times the difference between the two values, i.e.,
$\text{LR} = 2(-2341.7 + 2379.7) = 75.91.$

It has to be compared with a χ^2 distribution with two degrees of freedoms (the two coefficients for `WAGE` and `NO_CHILDREN` restricted to zero). The test statistic is much larger than the critical value at the 5%-level (p-value much smaller than 0.05). Therefore, the null hypotheses that all variables jointly have no significant explanatory power has to be rejected.

Hypothesis about Model Assumptions

2.3.8. a) The Ramsey RESET-test can be used to test the null hypothesis of a correct functional form. The general idea is to add higher order terms (e.g., squares of the predicted value of the dependent variable) as explanatory variables and to check whether they are jointly significant.

b) The null hypothesis cannot be rejected at the 5% level a the test statistic is below the critical value (the p-value is larger than 0.05). Consequently, one would continue with the linear model.

2.3.9. No sample solution.

2.3.10. a) Heteroskedasticity means that error variances are not constant, but might change across observations. For the specific application, the variance of error terms, i.e., the unexplained part in wages, might be higher for people with higher education. If all other assumptions are met, coefficient estimates are still consistent under heteroskedasticity. However, the estimates would not be efficient any more and the estimated standard errors might be wrong.

b)
- The null hypothesis of the White Test is H_0: error terms are homoskedastic. The idea of the test is to regress squared OLS residuals as a proxy of the error variances on a constant, the regressors, the squares, and cross products of the regressors to examine whether the test equation can significantly explain $\hat{u}_i^2$ which would imply heteroskedasticiy.
- No cross terms would imply that only the squares of the regressors would be in the test equation, i.e., $\texttt{SCHOOL\_T}^2$, $\texttt{AGE}^2$, $\texttt{SEX}^2$, and $\texttt{DEAST}^2$, resulting in only 4 degrees of freedom for the test (four coefficients should jointly be equal to zero); adding the variables and cross terms (except dummies), results in 16 degrees of freedom. Thus, the test was run in the version with cross terms.
- The test statistic is large implying that the explanatory variables can explain a significant part of the variance in squared residuals, which implies that the variance of error terms is not constant. The p-value is smaller than 0.0. Thus, the null hypothesis has to be rejected at the 5% level. We find evidence for the presence of heteroskedasticity.

2.3.11. One possible test is based on the Jarque-Bera Statistic, which compares the skewness and kurtosis of the empirical distribution of the residuals with the theoretical values of any normal distribution, which are 0 and 3, respectively. The test statistic is a weighted average of the departure of both moments and follows asymptotically a chi^2-distribution with 2 degrees of freedom. Consequently, The 95% quantile is given by 5.991.

An alternative test, Liliefor's test, is based on the maximum difference between the empirical distribution function of the residuals and the theoretical cumulative distribution function of a normal distribution with expected value and variance equal to those of the estimated residuals. This maximum difference does not follow a standard distribution, but critical values are tabulated.

2.3.12. a) Hint: No complex calculations are required. Focus on the information provided in the output.

b) The Durbin-Watson statistic is the only statistic referring to the error terms in the provided output. It is used for testing the null hypothesis of "no autocorrelation of first order". Given its value clearly below 1.6, the null hypothesis has to be rejected at the 5% level.

c) Autocorrelation of error terms might lead to biased estimates of coefficients. Furthermore, it will lead to biased estimates of the variance. Therefore, the t-statistics cannot be interpreted in the usual way by comparing it with an appropriate t- or approximate standard normal distribution.

d) Possible reasons are wrong functional form (including structural breaks) or missing variables (including dynamic components). Dependent on the source of autocorrelation, alternative strategies might be used to reduce or remove it.

2.3.13. a) No sample solution.

b) No sample solution.

c) Hint: Take the large size of the sample into account.

Model Selection

2.3.14. a) R^2 indicates the share of variation of y that can be explained by the variation of the explanatory variables x_k. You would choose the model with the highest R^2.

b) Adding further variables cannot decrease the R^2 even if they do not have any effect in the true model. Thus, the procedure risks to result in a model with a high number/share of irrelevant variables, while reducing the precision of the estimates.

c) Information criteria reflect the trade-off between good fit (low variance of the error terms) and number of parameters. Given a rather small number of $N = 65$ observations, the Akaike information criterion (AIC) might be preferred. In general, for sufficiently large samples, the consistent criteria BIC or HQ theoretically offer an advantage. For all information criteria, the selected model is the one with the smallest value.

2.3.15. a) Yes, they are nested as one can be obtained from the other by adding/subtracting a variable. The specification test is given by the test of statistical significance of the coefficient of `FULLTIME` in model 1. The corresponding t-statistic i 1.9177. Thus, the coefficient is not statistically significant different from zero at the 5% level (but it would be significant at the 10%). Consequently, one would select the simpler model with only `SEX` as explanatory variable.

b) The models are not nested.

c) Exceptionally, a comparison based on R^2 would be feasible as both models include the same number of explanatory variables. Based on the R^2, one would prefer model 2 due to the lager R^2. The more general approach consists in relying on an information criterion. Given the relative low number of observations, one might prefer AIC, but the also provided consistent Schwarz criterion (BIC) is also an admissible option. When comparing based on the AIC, the value is smaller for model 2, which would be the preferred choice. The same result is obtained when comparing the BIC values.

d) Results for the Durbin-Watson test are provided. If the null hypothesis of no autocorrelation is rejected for one model, but not for the other, one might prefer the model without autocorrelated errors. In the specific application, both models do not exhibit significant autocorrelation, as might have been expected for a cross-sectional analysis.

2.3.16. Endogeneity of a regressor implies that OLS estimates $\hat{\Theta}$ might be inconsistent, while the results of instrumental variable regression $\tilde{\Theta}$ would be consistent if all assumption regarding the instruments are satisfied. If there was no endogeneity, both estimators would be consistent. Under the null hypothesis of no endogeneity both estimators would be consistent, i.e., converge to the true parameters. It is also possible to calculate the asymptotic variance of the difference of both estimators (Var_H). The Hausman test statistic is given by

$$H = (\hat{\Theta} - \tilde{\Theta})'(\frac{Var_H}{N})^{-1}(\hat{\Theta} - \tilde{\Theta})$$

and follows asymptotically a χ^2 distribution with the number of degrees of freedom equal to the number of parameters in the model. If the difference between both estimators is small, the Hausman test statistic H will be small as well and the null hypothesis is not rejected. If there is endogeneity, the difference between the esimators might become large. Consequently, the H statistic is large and the null hypothesis has to be rejected.

4.4 Panel Data

2.4.1. a) In the cross-sectional setting, it is not necessary to contact the same firms in 2025, 2027, and 2029. However, it is necessary in the panel setting.

b) It is more difficult to collect panel data, since the interviewed firms have to be traced over time and are willing to answer the questions in all three years.

2.4.2. a) Note that the dependent variable is the logarithm of the hourly wage! If an individual has one more year of schooling, it can expect the logarithm of the hourly wage to be higher by about 0.1083 ceteris paribus, which corresponds to a 10.83% higher hourly wage.

b) No, the panel structure is not considered since the time series observations of the individuals are simply stacked, i.e., all observations are pooled to one sample. The model was estimated by OLS

c) The only test statistic shown in the output that refers to one of the standard assumptions is the Durbin-Watson statistic. Its value of 0.3479 is far below the critical value of 1.6. Thus, the null hypothesis of no autocorrelation of first order has to be rejected.

Hint: Think about the reason for finding autocorrelation in the pooled model given that the cross-sectional dimension is quite large ($N = 4,058$), while the time dimension is small ($T = 4$).

2.4.3. No sample solution.

2.4.4. a) The null hypothesis is H_0: RE estimator is consistent, i.e., there is no correlation between the explanatory variables and the random effects.

b) The test statistic is based on the comparison of the random and fixed effects estimators $\hat{\beta}_{RE}$ and $\hat{\beta}_{FE}$. Under the null hypothesis, both estimators are consistent, i.e., should be similar. If the sum of the squared differences weighted with an estimate of the inverse of the covariance matrix of the differences ($V(\hat{\beta}_{RE} - \hat{\beta}_{FE})$) becomes too large, the null hypothesis must be rejected.

$$H = (\hat{\beta}_{RE} - \hat{\beta}_{FE})'[V(\hat{\beta}_{RE} - \hat{\beta}_{FE})]^{-1}(\hat{\beta}_{RE} - \hat{\beta}_{FE})$$

c) The test statistic $H = 142.17$, which is much larger than the 95% quantile of the χ^2-distribution with four degrees of freedom (9.488). Consequently, the marginal probability is much lower than 5% and the null hypothesis has to be rejected at the 5% level. Therefore, the fixed effects estimator should be used.

2.4.5. No sample solution.

2.4.6. a) In the fixed effects model, the influence of all non time-varying variables is covered by the individual constant. Thus, introducing such variables into the model results in a lack of identification.

b) If the variable changes only for a few observations over time, the effect can be estimated. However, the size of the coefficient will reflect the influence on monthly wages when changing gender, but not the general gender gap, which is still covered by the fixed effects for all other observations.

c) The influence of non time-varying variables can be estimated in the random effects model. However, this will only be adequate if the conditions for random effects estimation are satisfied, in particular, no correlation between explanatory variables and individual specific effects.

2.4.7. a) No sample solution.

b) No sample solution.

c) Hint: Think about instrumental variables.

4.5 Discrete and Limited Dependent Variables

2.5.1. No sample solution.

2.5.2. Predictions of the Probit model always fall in the interval [0,1], i.e., can be interpreted as probabilities, while predictions of the Linear Probability Model might be negative or larger than one. Furthermore, there is no inherent heteroskedasticity in the Probit model.

2.5.3. a) Only the ratio (β/σ) affects the likelihood function and, consequently, is identified. If β and σ are multiplied by the same constant K, the ratio does not change. Hence, (β/σ) and $(K\beta/K\sigma)$ are observationally equivalent. Thus, β is identified only up to a scale and β and σ cannot be identified separately. To avoid this problem, σ is normalized to 1.

b) Maximizing the above likelihood function means choosing the $\hat{\boldsymbol{\beta}}$ that gives us the highest probability of generating the observed data. In case of a binary dependent variable, this means that we choose the parameters such that the probability of y_i taking the values we have observed is maximized. In the case of a Probit model, this implies that we choose $\hat{\boldsymbol{\beta}}_{ML}$ such that $\Phi(x_i, \hat{\boldsymbol{\beta}})$ (this is the estimated $Prob(y_i = 1)$) is large for the individuals i for whom $y_i = 1$ was observed, and small for those individuals i for whom $y_i = 0$ was observed.

After normalizing $\sigma = 1$, the log-likelihood function becomes:

$$l(\boldsymbol{\beta}) = \sum_{i=1}^{N} \left\{ y_i \cdot ln \left[\Phi \left(\boldsymbol{x}_i' \boldsymbol{\beta} \right) \right] + (1 - y_i) \cdot ln \left[1 - \Phi \left(\boldsymbol{x}_i' \boldsymbol{\beta} \right) \right] \right\}$$

Let us abbreviate $\Phi\left(\boldsymbol{x}_i'\boldsymbol{\beta}\right) = \Phi_i$. Then, the first order condition is:

$$\frac{l(\boldsymbol{\beta})}{\partial \boldsymbol{\beta}} = \sum_{i=1}^{N} \left\{ y_i \cdot \frac{\phi_i}{\Phi_i} \boldsymbol{x}_i + (1 - y_i) \cdot \frac{-\phi_i}{1 - \Phi_i} \boldsymbol{x}_i \right\}$$

where we have used

- the chain rule $[\Phi(x_i'\beta)]' = \Phi'(x_i'\beta)' = \phi * x_i$
- and the rule for logarithms $ln(f)' = \frac{f'}{f}$ and thus $ln(\Phi)' = \frac{\phi}{\Phi}$.

There is no closed formula available for the cumulative normal distribution Φ. Therefore, finding a solution to the first order conditions has to rely on numerical optimization methods.

2.5.4. a) $Y_i^* = \beta_0 + \beta_1 X_{1i} + \beta_2 X_{2i} + \beta_3 X_{3i} + \beta_4 X_{4i} + u_i$ and $Y_i = 1$ if $Y_i^* > 0$ and $Y_i = 0$ otherwise.

b) Yes, in a Probit model the sign of the coefficient can be interpreted. Since the coefficient is +0.3149, having a university degree increases the probability of being employed. If all assumptions about the model are satisfied, the effect is significantly different from zero as the z-Statistic is larger than 2 in absolute value (the p-value is lower than 0.05).

c) In general, a marginal effect is the impact of a small change of an explanatory variable on the dependent variable ceteris paribus. In the analyzed Probit model, marginal effects of number of years spent in school can be computed using the partial derivative of $Prob(Y_i = 1)$ with regard to the variable `SCHOOL_T`.

$$\frac{\delta E(Y_i)}{\delta X_{\texttt{SCHOOL\_T}}} = \frac{\delta Prob(Y=1)}{\delta X_{\texttt{SCHOOL\_T}}} = \frac{\delta \Phi(X_i'\beta)}{\delta X_{\texttt{SCHOOL\_T}}} = \phi(X_i'\beta)\beta_{\texttt{SCHOOL\_T}}$$

d) The test-statistic is computed as $LR = -2ln(l_R - l_{UR})$, where l_R is the restricted log-likelihood (`Restr. log likel.`) for the model without any explanatory variables besides the constant and l_{UR} is the log-likelihood (`Log likelihood`) of the estimated model. The test statistic will be large if the model including explanatory variables is better than the one relying solely on a constant, i.e., the LR-test tests for overall significance of the model (all variables jointly have an effect on the dependent variable).

Formally: $H_0 : \beta_i = 0$, for all $i > 0$ (for all variables except the constant). The test statistic of 5607.5 is large compared with the 95% quantile of the χ^2-distribution with 4 degrees of freedom (9.488). Therefore, the marginal probability also indicated in the last row of the output is very small, in particular, $Prob(LR) < 0.0001 < 0.05$. The null hypothesis that all explanatory variables jointly have no influence on the employment probability has to be rejected at the 5%-level.

e) Mc-Fadden $R^2 = 1 - l_{UR}/l_R = 1 - (-3173.338/(-5977.109)) = 0.4691$

2.5.5. a) For example, sales revenues, profit, and age of the firm might have a positive impact, while the debt ratio is expected to have a negative impact.

b) In this application, the interpretation as firm net value appears natural, as firms with a positive net value will survive, while those with a negative net value become insolvent.

c) Note that the u_i are standard normally distributed due to the identifying assumption that $\sigma_u^2 = 1$. Then, it follows:

$$\begin{aligned} E(y) &= 0 \times prob(y = 0) + 1 \times prob(y = 1) \\ &= prob(x_i'\beta + u_i > 0) = prob(u_i > -x_i'\beta) \\ &= prob(u_i < x_i'\beta) = \Phi(x_i'\beta) \end{aligned}$$

d)
- Yes, the sign of the coefficient can be interpreted directly. The negative sign indicates that a higher debt ratios are linked to lower survival probabilities.
- Yes, the null hypothesis that the debt ratio has no effect can be tested. Given the large sample size, the z-statistic provided in the output can be well approximated by a standard normal distribution if all other assumptions about the model are satisfied. Given that the absolute value of this test statistic is much larger than the critical value at the 5% level (1.968), and, consequently, the p-value is much lower than 0.05, the null hypothesis of no effect has to be rejected, i.e., a higher debt ratio has a statistically significant negative impact on survival probability ceteris paribus.
- Each element of the sum is the marginal effect of the debt ratio for a particular firm i. Therefore, the sum divided by then number of firms N is the mean marginal effect.

e)
- 785.
- It is used to "translate" estimated probabilities of firm survival into predicted actual survival or not, i.e., if $prob(y_i > 0.5)$ we assume survival for $C = 0.5$.
- The total number of correct predictions is 793 for the Probit model and 785 for the the naive model. There is a slight advantage of the Probit model. Alternatively, one could focus on the correct prediction of failures only, as these might be more relevant, e.g., for bank providing loans. For the failures, the Probit model has 44 correct predictions, while the naive model has 0 correct predictions. The outperformance of the naive model is more clear-cut for this measure.

2.5.6. a) Since $y_i^* = x_i'\hat{\beta} + \varepsilon_i$ and $(x_i'\hat{\beta} = 1)$, it follows that $y_i^* = 1 + \varepsilon_i$.
For $y_i = 0$:

$$P(y_i = 0) = P(y_i^* \leq 0) = P(1+\varepsilon_i \leq 0) = P(\varepsilon_i \leq -1) = \Phi(-1) = 0.1587.$$

The probabilities for the outcomes 1 and 2 are obtained analogously:

$$P(y_i = 1) = \Phi(-0.5) - \Phi(-1) = 0.1498 \text{ and}$$
$$P(y_i = 2) = 1 - \Phi(-0.5) = 0.6915\,.$$

b) No sample solution.

c) The first probability will shrink, the last increase, no statement is possible for the middle one, since a positive coefficient shifts probability towards higher outcome categories.

2.5.7. a) No sample solution.

b) No sample solution.

c) Note that the coefficients are reported as odds ratios. Consequently, a value of $0.55 < 1$ implies that higher economic knowledge, ceteris paribus, is linked to a lower probability of choosing law rather than economics, which is the benchmark option.

d) For the variable intrinsic motivation the odds ratios are above 1 (e.g. 2.61 for law and 2.07 for ENT). Again the comparison is with the benchmark option economics. Consequently, a higher intrinsic motivation for economics is linked to a higher probability of choosing other fields of study rather than economics.

2.5.8. Hint: Write down the formula for $E[y]$ for a censored normal distribution with censoring at zero. As the censoring threshold increases, the probability of uncensored observations ($\Phi(x'\beta/\sigma)$) falls, and $E[y]$ reacts less to x. Consequently, OLS will underestimate β while the Tobit model corrects for this bias.

2.5.9. A basic model for dealing with censored variables is the Tobit model. The idea of the model is dealing with censoring of y at a given threshold (e.g. at zero) using a latent variable, which is observed only for the uncensored cases. The estimation is done by maximum likelihood. A typical application example would be household expenditures for specific categories of consumption goods, which are either zero or positive, i.e., they are censored at zero. If censoring is substantial, OLS estimates would be biased, while the Tobit model provides consistent estimates.

2.5.10. Hint: Compare the estimated slopes (0.117 and 0.155) with the true value 0.5. Just using the value zero for the censored observations (model 1) or excluding them from the estimation (model 2) will result in estimates biased towards zero. The Tobit model avoids this bias.

2.5.11. No sample solution.

2.5.12. a) `MILLS_RATIO` is the inverse of Mill's ratio from the selection correction equation in Heckman's procedure (Heckit). Wages are only observed for employed women. Therefore, in a first step, a probit model for the employment decision is estimated (normalizing $\sigma = 1$). Let denote Φ the cumulated standard normal distribution and ϕ its density function. Using the abbreviation $\Phi_i = \Phi(x_i'\beta)$ and $\phi_i = \phi(x_i'\beta)$, the inverse Mills ratio is defined as

$$\frac{\phi_i}{\Phi_i} = \frac{\phi(x_i'\beta)}{\Phi(x_i'\beta)}.$$

Adding this term to the original model corrects for the selection bias.

b) The inverse of Mill's ratio should be included when the selection into the sample (being employed) is correlated with the error of the wage equation. If it is omitted in this case, the estimates suffer from sample selection bias and become inconsistent. In the application, the absolute value of the t-statistic of the variable is high indicating relevance of the variable. The correction is needed in this case.

References

Jüttler, Michael, Stephan Schumann, Nicolas Hübner and Benjamin Nagengast (2025). Economic competencies as part of 21st century skills and their relevance to predicting the choice of a study program. *Citizenship, Social and Economics Education* **24**(2-3), 182–214.

P. Winker, *Exercise Book Advanced Econometrics*,
https://doi.org/10.1007/978-3-662-74252-5

FSC
www.fsc.org
MIX
Papier | Fördert
gute Waldnutzung
FSC® C083411

Kolibri 360 GmbH
Ferdinand-Jühlke-Straße 7
99095 Erfurt, Deutschland
produktsicherheit@kolibri360.de